I0013117

THE Dx CULTURE CODE

How to use organizational culture to
drive Digital Transformation as your
competitive advantage

By Mayda Barsumyan

Abelian Academic
an imprint of
The Abelian Group
Saint Louis, Missouri, USA

Book Versions
Ingram ISBN: 978-1-950116-00-3
eBook ISBN: 978-1-950116-01-0
KDP Paperback ISBN: 978-1-950116-02-7

Cover Design By Mayda

© 2019 Mayda Barsumyan
Dx Culture Code is a registered trademark.

All rights reserved. No part of this book may be reproduced in any form without prior written permission from the publisher. This work represents the views and opinions of the author alone. No liability in conjunction with the content or the use of ideas connected with this work is assumed by the publisher.

CONTENTS

FOREWORD
by David Finkel

Wall Street Journal bestselling Co-author of, SCALE: 7 Proven Principles to Grow Your Business and Get Your Life Back

Have you ever felt like the world was moving so very fast? Changes in technology and the ways we interact – as consumers and creators – have left many of us reeling.

For over twenty years I've written about how to succeed in business. My company has coached thousands of companies to grow faster and become more durable. Over that time millions of business leaders, entrepreneurs, and executives have read my syndicated column or previous books. Yet I still find myself struggling to keep pace with the changing world.

Just earlier this week I spent several hours reading a cache of articles I had flagged for review describing a new technology that is an open-source tool that will literally transform a core part of our business. Three months ago, I didn't even know that this technology existed, and now here I was, having to recalibrate our company strategy in light of what this new platform promised.

Does that feel familiar to you?

I know our clients struggle with this same dilemma.

Many times I've found myself wishing for a simple map laying out the guiding principles and best practices to help my company and team effectively navigate this digital transformation. I'm not talking about what technologies are about to break out at this moment, or what new trend is about to explode. What I craved was something more fundamental. In a world that is moving so fast what I needed was something that was enduring, something that provided a concrete framework to make sense of the dizzying change we are all struggling to cope with clear.

What you have here is that map.

The Dx Culture Code is a simple blueprint of how not just to keep pace with the blur of technology, but to actually use this time in history to make simple shifts to encode the best of what this digital transformation offers into the DNA of your culture.

Written by an extremely intelligent and farsighted thinker, Mayda Barsumyan, this book will give you the foundation to rethink how you bring technology into the heart of your company. This is not a static decision, but rather a dynamic process that you'll revisit again and again. And Mayda has mapped out this process for us and stepped forward as our guide to make this critical shift.

I originally met Mayda five years ago when her company became a business coaching client of my firm. Since that time, I've watched with amazement the way she has scaled her ideas and impacted some of the most successful companies in the world. She has something important to say, and The Dx Culture Code is will help you rethink the role of technology, culture, systems, and people in your organization.

For you to succeed, you need to get this right. The stakes are extremely high. This book will help you get it right.

David Finkel

Wall Street Journal bestselling Co-author of, SCALE: 7 Proven Principles to Grow Your Business and Get Your Life Back

ACKNOWLEDGMENTS

A big thank you to all my ERP and digital transformation clients for the opportunity to serve your organization. Your incredible projects created the space for me to utilize my expertise and stretch my thinking.

This book is in memory of my mom – a resilient, philanthropic, independent woman. I am grateful for the leadership and confidence she instilled in me.

Most of all, thank you to my teenage twins, Edward and Ezabelle, for being supportive throughout my career and for sitting in many boardrooms (AKA "bored rooms") with me.

To all my rooted sisters and friends, thank you for standing by me no matter what.

Thank you to my friend, Cornelia for staying up many nights and help me with editing and publishing of the book.

Thank you to Lethia Owens and her amazing team. Without their guidance and encoragement, this book would not have been written.

Thank you to my brother and his family for their consistent encouragement over the years.

MEET MAYDA

Mayda Barsumyan Advisor, Author, Speaker

Mayda Barsumyan, CEO and founder of iTransfluence a Digital Transformation Company focused on Transforming Communities, Organizations and Individuals Worldwide through Technology and Leadership Principles. She is a globally-recognized leader on digital business strategy, known for her pioneering work on using the organizational culture to drive digital transformation. Mayda is author of "The Dx Culture Code" .

For over 25 years Mayda has been in the trenches working in all positions of technology gaining insight and knowledge, as well as creating formulas to take organizations to a level of global proportions.

From her work in the public sector to private and nonprofit organizations she has uncovered common threads that can be detrimental to the downfall of growth and potentially the death of the organization.

Mayda brings a unique combination of technology brilliance and innovation strategies into the heartbeat of cultural development so an organization is foundationally built for digital transformation.

Mayda has consulted and developed custom Blueprints for upgrades, implementations, and system modernization for Fortune 500 companies such as Boeing, NAPA, Centene, Oracle; Public Sector Organizations such as the State of California, City of Kansas City; Nonprofits such as Ascension Health, East Kentucky Power; Financial Services such as Prudential Reinsurance, Pacific Life; and many others. Currently, in addition to providing consulting services, Mayda is serving as interim Chief Digital Transformation Officer for companies that need digital leadership, but do not have that person internally.

Her passion for making a positive change in the world using digital transformation is a mission that goes back to her roots in the beginning of her career.

For more tools and content from Mayda, visit

MaydaBarsumyan.com.

INTRODUCTION

It feels like it was a lifetime ago, but I can recall the very place I was standing and I'm sure you can too. On the morning of September 11, 2001, I was heading into the office as usual, but on this particular morning I was running later than I had anticipated. I had just acquired a new client, and my head was spinning with a list of to-do's for the day to come. I was driving on autopilot, headed on I-80 eastbound from New Jersey to Manhattan, when something made me stop on my tracks.

A heavy yellowish-gray streak hung in the sky. "A cloud?," I wondered to myself ... *"On this perfectly clear day?"*

As I sat forward in the seat to look and focus my eyes, it became clear to me that I was looking at a massive plume of smoke. On any other day, looking out at the skyline of Manhattan, a layer of smog gathered at the tops of the buildings wouldn't have seemed all that out of place. However, on this day, the protrusion of this ominous thunderhead against a clear blue sky made it clear that something terrible had happened.

I fumbled with clammy hands to turn on the radio. *"Two planes have collided into the World Trade Center ..." I gasped in utter disbelief.*

The words coming out of my radio felt nostalgic like an old-fashioned radio broadcast. Surely this was fiction, it couldn't be real - and then as traffic continued to crawl closer to I-95, I saw it ... the south tower of the World Trade Center collapsed before my very eyes.

From my distant vantage point, it looked almost as though the tower was swaying, then as if its knees had buckled below it, disappearing into nothing. An emptiness briefly appeared in the New York City skyline, quickly replaced by an epic cloud of smoke, dust and debris that seemed to swallow my city whole. At this stage the north tower continued to smoke.

I looked down at my radio – it was 9:58 a.m.

I returned to autopilot driving mode. This time, without that gnawing list of action items in my head. For the first time in my life, there was just silence – an absence of thought.

Somehow, I arrived at my office that morning. I couldn't tell you how; what route I took, or what time I arrived. I walked into work and found an eerie silence and hushed tones. I heard someone crying down the hall.

Everyone was gathered in the cafeteria. They were watching the attack on the Twin Towers and the collapse replay over and over again on the television. They were trying to process the events of the morning just as I was, a task that seemed nearly impossible. I sat down with my coworkers, the executive team, and our peers in silence – everyone equal in their grief, despite their stature in the business.

No one knew quite what to say.

Thirty minutes later, I realized I should call my parents. I worked at the towers on a somewhat regular basis, and it wasn't uncommon to find me there a few times a month. We had clients whose headquarters were based in the buildings that had collapsed. I knew my parents would be worried. I sat down at my desk and tried to place a call to Bulgaria. A voice came over the line, *"We're sorry. All circuits are busy now. Please try your call again later."* The lines were overloaded.

In the days and weeks that followed, we struggled with grief in new ways. We suffered a collective loss as a community. Many of us suffered deeply personal losses of family members and friends.

At the office, we tried to find our way back to normal, but conversations would start around the watercooler or in the kitchen, and in a matter of seconds, it felt like it was Tuesday morning all over again.

People naturally sought out the comfort of their coworkers and work friends as they grappled with questions like:

How do we comfort those who lost loved ones?

How do we comfort and care for the children left behind?

How do we help clients, colleagues, families and friends stranded amidst the confusion and wreckage just out of our view from the Jersey shoreline?

Being so close, yet a body of water away, gave us a unique and terrible vantage point. We considered the implications and struggles from our relative comfort of our office just miles away.

The Culture Code is born.

In light of the enormous tragedy we'd endured personally, and as a community, we felt that we needed to shift our focus to the future, to what was left, to ensuring there would be a future for our children.

As you might imagine, this experience provided me with a unique perspective on what it takes to find true success in business – an unexpected gift in the face of unimaginable tragedy.

On the whole, our team felt that the best contribution we could make was to use our professional talents and abilities to help in the recovery.

We wanted to do our part to get our economy in order. The World Trade Center had been the home of industry giants in insurance, banking, communications, and government. These companies suffered catastrophic losses of their key employees, data, servers, and more. The long-term recovery and viability of these organizations would be dependent on their response to these losses in those early hours; how they handled the loss of their people, processes and systems.

As we navigated the disaster both personally and professionally, we saw that the organizations that ultimately survived – and even thrived – in the aftermath of this event knew that they had to focus their efforts on four key areas immediately:

1. Their People

2. Their Culture

3. Their Processes

4. Their Systems

I discovered that corporate culture was at the heart of it all. An organization's corporate culture determined how successfully they managed through each of these four areas, and how well they fared in the aftermath.

Moving through my career and my life in the years that have followed, I have taken the lessons I learned through this experience to heart. They have been in my head and heart in every new client meeting, and in every stage of my own businesses growth. I have been able to look at business, technology, and success in new ways, thanks to the observations and experiences I learned. I now want to share this way of thinking with you. I want to help you learn how to look at every facet of your business through a lens that will build sustainability.

In this book, I will introduce you to The Dx Culture Code, a new way of looking at business, leadership and the movement of Digital Transformation. We will explore the most common and significant business issues leaders are facing today, and we will apply the lens of The Culture Code to navigating these issues. We will look at how to incorporate culture and focus on people, processes and systems which will help a business move forward, no matter what their circumstance. While reading this book, or when you have a moment of break-through applying these core elements into your company, know that you can reach out to me at DxCultureCode.com. I actively consult, teach, and speak for organizations who want to propel themselves forward in business.

Part One:

AWARENESS

AWARENESS

Chapter One:
The Emergence of the Dx Culture Code

The DNA of Digital Transformation began to emerge in 1999 while I was in a meeting. I was working in the European division of Booz-Allen and Hamilton, and we were preparing for the transition to the Euro. In 1999, the big multinationals were just discovering they'd need new systems to comply with the Euro's statutory reporting requirements.

What they needed was something that didn't exist yet, a systematic triangulation process. I will not bore you with the details, but triangulation involves converting one national currency to another by way of a third currency, for example, the Euro. Today, triangulation is part of every financial system, but in 1999 this concept was untested.

No one knew how it would work, but it was quickly becoming obvious that every foreign organization would need it.

What I liked about working at Booz-Allen and Hamilton was being surrounded by geniuses. Geniuses on the business side, as well as geniuses in technology. Their expertise leads us to be the first to invent new tools and bring them to the market.

This meeting in 1999 was filled with those geniuses, but as often as it happens in a room full of smart people, the group had gotten stuck on how best to solve the triangulation problem. The purpose of this meeting was to refine the code, but it wasn't working; I'd update the configuration, and it would crash. And crash again. Everyone was getting frustrated.

That's when one of the managing partners happened to walk in.

We updated him on the problem, talked a bit back and forth about solutions, and as he prepared to leave, he turned back and said: *"You will figure it out. You're true Booz-Allenians."*

And at that moment, we gained the confidence and clarity we needed as a group to move forward and solve the problem at hand.

What had this partner done in those few words? He'd connected our technological task with our cultural commitments. He was referring to the organization that we knew so well.

At Booz-Allen, individual passions build upon each other within a highly collaborative environment, as seen with the five values that align with the purpose statement:

- Unflinching courage
- Passionate service
- Ferocious integrity
- Collective ingenuity
- Champion's heart

Collectively, we celebrate the ideas and ingenuity of our people, the purpose that drives what we do each day, and the passion with which we serve our clients, communities, and colleagues.

The next day, with fresh energy to push us forward, we fixed the code and completed testing.

That code and that technology are now being used in the majority of the financial systems around the world today.

What I learned from my time at Booz-Allen was this: lasting organizational change can only take place at the confluence of technology and culture.

This book is intended to spur you and your company forward. To act as a guide in becoming a digital technology company. This is relevant for so-called transforming companies adopting digital technology as well as for those born around digital technology. This book is useful for both, because the goal of each type of company is the same: every company must be a digital technology company. The digital technology company has become the universal business; all other businesses are already, or will become, applications or extensions of the basic idea of the digital technology company.

In reading this book, you will have direct access to more than two decades of my personal, practical experience of Digital Transformation, and access to a much wider set of theoretical knowledge and practical experience through other sources. This book is designed to start a process of changing how you think about what a business organization is, and how humans and technology interact to achieve business goals. It empowers anyone to create a culture of Digital Transformation – one who anticipates, responds to, and initiates changes in digital technology and its applications in human organizations.

My conviction that Digital Transformation is the key to the marketplace of the present, and the future, is the driving force that led me to write this book. I desire to help leaders understand that Digital Transformation driven by organizational culture must be a central part of their business strategy. Business success is no longer simply about delivering technological advances; it is about providing a smoother experience for customers, better products and services, and improved processes to create a more efficient organization. Furthermore, Digital Transformation is now more about people than ever before. Staff within any organization are the main drivers for change. Information Technology staff have revolutionized their roles within organizations. They no longer simply fix issues and sustain the functionality of business operating systems. IT specialists are now facilitators of change within the organization. Thus, they are now a key component of business strategy. Digital Transformation has evolved from being solely technology-focused to becoming more about people and their contributions, and then about the interface between people and technology. Modern Digital Transformation inspires staff and invests in their skill-sets to give them the opportunity to empower and change the whole organization.

Through these next nine chapters we will walk through the cycle of Digital Transformation (Dx); Awareness, Awakening, and Action. We'll discuss real-world examples of how businesses across a myriad of industries have successfully transformed their cultures, and their teams, into true Digital Technology Companies and abandoned an obsolete view that they have "settled" with their static technology. We'll share the myths that act as hurdles to Dx and teach you the hacks your company needs to fight for your future. Trust me, don't stop in the sand. The sea of your potential is waiting on the other side.

Chapter Two:

Digital Transformation Isn't Just About Technology

Organizations do not succeed in Digital Transformation, unless their soul is digital. "Being Digital" as an organization is the key.

The goal of Digital Transformation is creating a culture of permanent Digital Transformation.

The Dx Leader

This isn't the book I would have written ten years ago.

Ten years ago, the conversation was about finance, operational and management transformation. Growing through technology was a foreign concept. Companies were still focused on investing in salespeople to grow their organization.

But that's not the conversation we need to have today.

Today the conventional sales people are replaced with lead generation engines. The formula for success is not only having a system that works, but also a simple system.

My clients tell me that they want their products to be "Amazon-like." "We do not need a manual to navigate in Amazon," they say, "You just place your order. You know what to do."

Today, all financial systems should be just as easy to use. No training should be needed.

Why am I very successful in helping my clients elevate their companies through technology? Because I understand this elegantly complex concept: the need for Digital Transformation and all the factors that drive it.

This lesson became clear when I was traveling home from Atlanta a few years ago, and my phone rang. It was my friend David.

David owns a company that manufactures and sells pure essential oils for health and cooking.

David was doing so well: unbelievable profits, excellent products, expert management ... his company was amazing. I'd always admired David – I had learned so much from him about building sustainable organizations – so I was shocked when he told me he faced a dilemma.

When he started the company, he basically owned the market. There was little to no competition, and scaling was easy. But now with new technology and new online sales channels, his price had to go down. He was selling more to wholesalers, who could go to his competition at any time. His old processes weren't prepared for such a change.

David was worried.

"Mayda," I remember him saying, *"I have to do something with all this new tech, or I won't have a company for very much longer. What is that 'something' I need to do? My staff has so many ideas, but I feel overwhelmed just by listening. Where do I start?"*

The next day I got on a plane and went to see David.

We brainstormed for the entire day. David understood the importance of technology, but most essentially he understood now the importance of his leadership in fostering a culture of technological innovation.

Fast forward seven months. My team gave David the leadership direction, and together we broke the silos of his organization and built an integrated system. We also offered an internal collaboration platform to clients.

The new visibility of his products, plus the new services and client experience we created, were crucial for the unprecedented growth his company has experienced in the years following this technological transformation.

Society is in a state of permanent disruption. This is due in part to the rapid development of computer-driven technologies. Cloud computing. The Internet of Things. Automation. Digital technology has lowered the barrier to entry into business for many sectors causing a democratization that has changed the entire landscape.

The ease with which users interact with new complex technologies has made it possible to attract customers through precisely these new technologies. There are new banks which offer their services only online, coffee shops where the only worker is a robotic arm, the delivery service powered by fleets of self-navigating vehicles, or the use of intelligent systems which replace actuaries in insurance companies. The growth of this list is accelerating steadily, and the impact is clear: Businesses which have not adapted to new technologies have disappeared. Out of all the Fortune 500 companies active in the year 2000, only around 48% were still active in 2017; moreover, in almost any given sector, a small number of companies control two-thirds or more of the market share.1 However, successful companies do not simply use new technologies. They engage in and direct their own process of Digital Transformation.

Digital Transformation (Dx) as an all-pervasive characteristic of a successful business works for businesses that are adapting to new digital technologies step by step, and for businesses that are *"born digital." "Born digital"* businesses are based on constant technological and organizational change throughout the entire organization. This new approach to doing business requires a culture which makes business activities consist of pieces which can be modified quickly to deploy new ideas, respond to changes in markets and supply chains, and work with other digital sectors to reach new markets.

The basic model of a business working on the premises of Digital Transformation is this: business processes are built from modules, which can be purchased from a vendor and customized to work together. This modularity allows for maximum flexibility. Modules can be modified, added, omitted, or made larger or smaller quickly. This is the technological key to adaptability. The business itself spends as few resources as possible in building the technology it needs and at the same time is devoting more resources to product development, production, and marketing.

However, Digital Transformation must be permanent. Simply having a modular design means little. At present, digital technologies must function within a human organization. The organization itself must have a culture of Digital Transformation in order to apply the technology successfully.

I worked for over two decades selling software configuration to businesses. My main task was tuning enterprise software to meet a client's business structure. There were always two key assumptions: 1.) the software and the structure of the client company were separate, and 2.) any software solution was a static one ... once the software was up and running, the transformation was complete.

The business or government agency, who was my customer, improved its efficiency, recovered a lot of cash from operations, improved revenue forecasts – and consigned itself to a road leading to obsolescence, high future costs in technology investment, and, in some cases, outright extinction.

The static software upgrade is of a bygone era Looking forward, it is my firm conviction that all the goals involved in delivering a product, which is the entirety of its organizational activity, derive from one and only one fundamental goal:

The fundamental goal of any Digital Transformation is bringing about a culture of permanent Digital Transformation.

Thus, executives must follow this mantra:

My business is a digital-human culture in permanent transformation. My calling is to champion, cultivate, and curate that culture.

The most effective Digital Transformations happen spontaneously, at any level of the organization. This means that digital leadership must be flat: every member must be empowered to seek out new technology, be transformed by it, and share this transformation with others. Through this process, it is possible for a company to remain aware and adaptable.

It is necessary to have the conditions in place for these transformations to occur, take hold, and improve efficiency. I believe that the key to this is not the technology itself, but how to grow an organization which thinks and reacts technologically.

It is important to understand how to drive Digital Transformation across your organization and identify the characteristics of a successful Digital Transformation strategy. A decade ago, we may never have thought it to be true, but technology is beginning to take a back seat to business strategy. Digital Transformation now requires business strategists to be audacious and adaptable in their leadership and decision-making. Unfortunately, many businesses are only prepared to maintain the status quo when it comes to digital technology. They are not ready to go the way of Digital Transformation. They are likely to fall behind while their competitors become disruptors in the marketplace.

Business leaders see clearly that having an effective Digital Transformation strategy drives digital maturity for organizations. Without such an effective Digital Transformation strategy, businesses risk losing their ability to change and adapt to the current and future market situations. The necessary level of flexibility is only possible by having and following a Digital Transformation strategy closely. An effective Digital Transformation strategy allows organizations to continue to innovate even as the technology continues to evolve around them.

The Digital Shift – Why Digital Transformation Matters

Digital Transformation has seen an incredible shift over the last decade. Traditionally, at the turn of the twenty-first century, Digital Transformation was viewed as the transfer of raw data into technological devices, such as computers and hard drives. However, today, Digital Transformation has transcended far beyond this model. It has shifted to become a very real and powerful source of competitive advantage for businesses and an integral and essential component of creating an effective and successful business strategy.

The key strategic components that enable and enhance gaining this advantage are the following:

1. Online User Experience: Digital Transformation can boost online capabilities for the users. Whether your business provides products or services, the process involves catering effectively to customers at each point along the customer's journey. Businesses must ask themselves how they can effectively employ technology and invest in certain areas of the customer's journey to increase customer conversions and retain customer loyalty. If businesses can utilize technology to increase their conversions by ten percent per year, they are going to grow their market share quickly and uncover new opportunities.

The key technologies in Digital Transformation are known by the acronym **SMACIT**. These technologies have become integral to the digital shift:

- Social

- Mobile

- Analytics

- Cloud

- Internet of Things

Management must identify how each of these technologies will enhance the user experience and provide a source of competitive advantage over their competition.

A classic example of a firm that was an early adopter of SMACIT technologies is McDonald's. How did this fast- food giant adopt Digital Transformation early on? As a restaurant, they were one of the first places to offer unencumbered Wi-Fi for their customers. By offering convenient and free-of-charge Wi-Fi for their customers, they were able to obtain important information about the demographics of their customers, their consumption patterns, and consumer behaviors. Then they were able to use that information to market effectively towards this demographic in the future. It provided McDonald's with a clear and real source of competitive advantage and a key strategy to staying one step ahead of their competition.

2. Enterprise-Wide Empowerment: Digital Transformation significantly extends the capabilities of members of an organization. Information and technology experts are now integral to business strategy decisions. Digital Transformation has empowered these staff members to become industry disruptors and game-changers for their organization. Business strategy evolves from a collaboration between digital technology professionals and operations management. IT staff work closely with the business strategy to optimize their abilities to provide innovative technologies.

3. Research and Development: Research and development of digital technology within the organization is a crucial component of Digital Transformation. With this empowerment, IT staff are now developing and evolving their work environment. There is now far more room for creativity, the development of new ideas, and the testing of technologies. This is the heart of a technologically-aware organization. As we will see again later, organizations that do not continue to invest in research and development will quickly become stagnant and be disrupted by their competition. Furthermore, business leaders are more readily investing in re-tooling and up-skilling their staff. Building the capabilities of an organization internally results in boosting output and improving organizational culture. It also means that when change is needed, the organization no longer has to look outside its own four walls – and can adapt quickly, saving a lot of time and cost in the long run.

4. Products and Services: Digital Transformation also matters because it has developed how products and services are now offered. This is the single biggest source of competitive advantage for organizations. If businesses can change the way their product or service is offered through technology, they have the opportunity to propel themselves quickly to a position of industry leadership. So, which firms have taken advantage of this type of digitalization?

Apple is a great example of using product digitalization. The iPhone is perhaps the single greatest example of digital product transformation we have experienced so far in the twenty-first century. Apple entirely disrupted the cellular phone industry by altering how the product was offered. The iPhone provided an all-in-one Smartphone package. The ramifications of this product transformation have been huge. With ongoing research and development of the product, the iPhone has also managed to disrupt the music industry, the camera industry, and the gaming industry, as well as many others, simply by developing and continuing to create amazing apps. Apples continued investment into Digital Transformation has allowed the company to revolutionize their business and stay at the forefront of the technology industry.

5. Business Processes: Digital Transformation also matters because it has the ability to transform business processes. Improved business processes allow organizations to reduce cost and increase overall business efficiency.

"Organizations are faced every day with the challenge to produce more and spend less. To grow, managers look for a way to improve their business processes in a way that results in cost reduction and awareness of what each process represents in the business." 2

How then does Digital Transformation reduce costs? The most significant area of savings is achieving savings through the automation of business processes. Automation allows a level of stability, reliability, and speed for organizations. The testing of data, analytics, operating systems, and outputs are all made more efficient. An increase in efficiency means that more time and energy can be spent on other areas of business operations such as research and development technologies.

Effective business automation must be enterprise-wide. One legacy process can effectively negate business automation. There are many anecdotes which illustrate this all-or-nothing principle. One which I often recount involves a company which had decided to automate all of its treasury and financial activities. However, for reasons which became clear only in hindsight, one office's expense reimbursements were not included in the automation. This was a small office, staffed by someone who had been with the company in this role for fifteen years. As a result, this person was manually entering account information into a separate spreadsheet, disconnected from the rest of the financial software. It was later discovered that this employee had been forging expenses. It turns out that this person was personally involved with a middle manager, who in the preparatory phase had shielded this expense department from being integrated into the system. The scheme was eventually discovered when the manager left the company, and both were prosecuted for embezzlement.

If there had been first, a culture of Digital Transformation, such a loophole would have been nearly impossible: no one would have allowed any part of the company not to be incorporated in any business process implementation. Digitizing the operations of only one part of the organization will almost certainly cause a number of bottlenecks which will be immediately painful. I was involved in an implementation, in which the client was convinced that only digitization of treasury operations justified the expense of digitization. Their argument was that the company was profitable, and that the profit margin did not justify the cost of changing the supply chain.

Despite my strong warnings, the client remained firm. As promised, management had access to a real-time view of the financials of the company, at least in the treasury department. As promised, they could see in real time that they were saving cash, but it was a small fraction of the projected sum. It took another two months of manual investigation of all the accounts to understand where cash was still trapped. The real problem in the company was not treasury, but in the supply chain. Of course, management should have realized that their industry was heavily dependent on obtaining good contracts with suppliers, and that waste in this area had the potential to eliminate competitive advantage. The matter was rectified – old KPIs were replaced with more relevant measurements; nationwide accounts, licensing agreements, and vendor contracts were re-negotiated, yielding savings equaling around twenty percent of the operating budget, but the final solution cost much more than it should have. In a culture of Digital Transformation, the cost of a digital solution would have taken the bottlenecks into account, and thus would have been applied to the entire enterprise.

The Cost of Doing Nothing

The above example is a cautionary tale: no response, even in a profitable business position, is fatal. Digital Transformation has become so important; there are now large costs associated with businesses that do not develop and follow through with a Digital Transformation strategy. The cost of doing nothing puts an organization at risk of becoming technologically stagnant. Without making advancement in the five areas mentioned above, businesses face the very real possibility of being disrupted and overtaken by their competition. As a result, businesses that don't keep up or lead in this area may find themselves obsolete within a short period of time.

The characteristic of Digital Transformation that makes it compelling for all organizations to invest in, is that it is relevant across every single business sector and every single industry.

Airbnb and Uber are the ultimate examples of how Digital Transformation has completely disrupted the hotel and private transport industries. They exemplify to other players in their industries the costs of doing nothing. Taxi drivers and hotel owners all over the world have seen their industry dramatically shift because of the service transformation these organizations have implemented. Those businesses in the private transport and accommodation industry that do not adapt and embrace Digital Transformation are quickly finding themselves more and more obsolete.

The costs of doing nothing are also visible in the print industries.

Recent years have seen radical changes in how we now consume our news; the younger generations access nearly all their news digitally. The newspaper and journal industries are in the middle of product digitalization and disruption that this sector has never encountered before. Organizations involved in this industry must invest in evolving their technologies or die.

Leading a Culture of Digital Transformation

In a culture of permanent transformation, everyone must lead. Executives may be those who take the first step, and who have oversight over the effective monitoring of Digital Transformation. They are the standard-bearers of this ethos, but the culture must be built into the activity of every member. This aspect of management requires a flat structure, in which communication moves without obstacles to everyone. Seeking out better ways to implement technology to accomplish tasks should be the one and only job description of each person in the company. The rest is an extension of that principle to the scope of the goal each person has.

While not everyone is a strong leader at the outset, Digital Transformation should be the occasion to strengthen organizational skills in each person. In this way, investing in technology is an investment in human development. Executives must choose to relinquish their authority and empower managers to act as facilitators of enterprise-wide innovation which originates with members working at the endpoints where the product is created, manufactured, marketed, sold, and distributed.

Digital Transformation also requires business leaders to have a high level of fearlessness and courage. Leaders must be adaptable and flexible in their decision-making. This means having the courage to change the direction of the business as soon as the technology necessitates it or as soon as the technology provides an opportunity to do so. Digital Transformation relies on a certain level of disruption in an industry for organizations to stay ahead of their competition. Business leaders are only able to do this by taking advantage of opportunities that arise and by being bold.

This type of leadership is often directly related to organizational culture. A strong, open culture is systematic to creativity and boldness in decision-making. Conversely, a weaker culture is more likely to create division amongst staff, there will be less buy-in, and business leaders will not have the conviction to carry through bold decisions. Creating a strong organizational culture does not happen overnight. Business leaders must begin this by encouraging open and honest communication throughout the business. It is the interactions between the people within the organization that can deliver real change.

Focusing on Strategy instead of Technology

Healthcare is one of the industries I specialize in.

Often, my clients call me to help out with an issue they are having. It can range from, *"I have problems with the Epic system, and my operations are at a standstill,"* to *"My major implementation project has failed. What can I do to get it up and running?"*

In this case, I knew the CFO. Ann and I were great friends and saw each other often at various healthcare events. Ann called me one morning and requested we see each other. The atmosphere in her office was amazingly welcoming, with flowers everywhere, but clearly, something was wrong. Ann had an issue with her billing.

They had just implemented a new billing system, and the coding was wrong. So wrong, in fact, her people couldn't use the system at all, and had to resort to manual billing.

The team was overwhelmed and, as you can imagine, could not bill fast enough.

It was an <u>EPIC FAIL</u> in every sense.

It took months of labor for us to fix the coding and the configuration. Finally, they were up and running again but not without a painful and costly lesson.

Afterward, Ann and I sat down to regroup. We discussed how to take strategic advantage of the technology we'd just implemented. I recommended that she consider improving the customer experience and offer self-service. She agreed.

In Phase II of our project, we implemented a customer portal where patients could not only view their bills and pay online, but also collaborate with their physicians and conduct research online.

I've been beating this drum for years, and although many of you now take this sort of online engagement as second nature, a few years ago it sounded to most people in health care like something from Star Trek!

But it's just one example of how using the right technology can take your work and your customer experience to the next level.

When the barrier between the organization and technology is allowed to fall, there is no distinction between digital awareness and the formulation of strategic objectives. The traditional view is that a business must invest in technology to maintain a competitive edge, specifically in reducing costs. They must have a digital strategy which somehow ties in to overarching goals.

This raises the perennial questions in business: How do these organizations focus on strategy? What are the criteria of a sound digital strategy? How is the digital strategy incorporated into the everyday running of an organization?

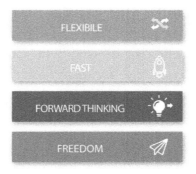

In a culture of Digital Transformation, these questions are eliminated. The digital technology is the strategy. The product or service to be produced is inseparable from the means of its production. Digital Transformation, being permanent, is the framework in which the business acts.

The key aspects of this culture are the Four Fs:

- Flexible

- Fast

- Forward Thinking

- Freedom

Let's take a closer look at these Four Fs ...

Flexible: Organizational leaders must incorporate flexibility into their digital strategy. This means implementing a variety of steps and methods that encourage frequent change to occur within the organization. When change is allowed to occur more often, the business takes on a certain fluidity, which makes it more adaptable. The more that change occurs, the easier it becomes for the organization to pivot and make technological advancements.

Furthermore, staff become comfortable with change and being challenged – meaning with each successive change, more progress is made. Modularity and scalability are two properties of a robust digital culture. One logistics company with whom I partnered had set out on the path of Digital Transformation. It realized that its technology allowed it to scale up its operations quickly. It decided to enter the manufacturing logistics market in China. With a modular design in which technology components were supplied through vendors, rather than being owned, I was able to add a manufacturing module to their cloud-based solution, seamless with the existing operations. Given that the company had embraced Digital Transformation, technological and human changes took place in harmony, resulting in an experience which was of great benefit for the company both in terms of revenue and in terms of human development.

Fast: Organizational leaders must also ensure their digital strategy is fast-paced. Speed is crucial to making and implementing technological changes. If a new technology is being introduced, a swift uptake by your organization is the only way to retain a competitive advantage. If your technological advancement is successful, imitators will be hot on your heels. An organization that has speed central to its strategy can create a sustained competitive advantage. Does your business have the skills to implement new technologies swiftly and effectively? Remember, often with Digital Transformation and the release of new technologies you only have one chance to impress your end user. Customers are becoming more and more fickle with how they judge success. The speed at which you implement your project and scalability may well define its success.

I helped a client using over 200 small tools for ERP, manufacturing, order management, among many other applications. Plus many processes were still executed manually. Changes in regulatory compliance required them to have a single platform within a short period of time or face sanctions. This included replacing reports with dashboard analytical tools and actionable tasks. Over 100 of these tools were replaced, all manual processes were automated, and a social communication network was implemented. The company saw a savings of five million dollars in the first year alone. However, management viewed this as a one-time, static solution. Once the changes had taken place, and the users were trained, the transformation came to an end. Ten years ago, this was an adequate deployment of digital technology. How well they will fare moving forward depends on whether they can make the transformation from a static solution to embracing constant technological innovation.

Forward Thinking: A culture of Digital Transformation must plan for potential changes in technology in every decision it makes. There are many examples of poor planning in organizations which view digital technology as merely another tool in the means of production. Modern organizations are far more sophisticated, but still, unless everyone is focused on the way they use technology to achieve organizational and operational goals, costly and avoidable mistakes will continue to take place. Instead of asking, where must this organization be in five years, the correct question is, where will the digital technology be in five years, and how will it define what this organization will be?

Technology may make it possible to shift industries altogether if the organization planned a response to potential technological disruption. It may make partnering with previously disconnected sectors possible, leading to greater market visibility. It may mean the difference between having to be acquired by another company or leading a merger or acquisition. In short, simply implementing a technological tool is insufficient. One must be in a position to acquire and discard tools as necessary. Again, modularity, owning as little technology as possible and instead creating a company of experts who know when to pick up and when to discard a given tool, makes it possible to plan with greater depth farther into the future.

Freedom: Business leaders must allow for freedom in their strategy. What does freedom mean? It means having the ability to react to what is in front of you. It means not forcing the business into rigid structures and processes. It means embracing change and being comfortable with the uncomfortable volatility in your working environment, because Digital Transformation operates effectively when businesses are comfortable in this zone.

Digital change is like fire. It is unpredictable, can spread quickly, and if you are not prepared, it can cause devastation to a business. Treating Digital Transformation as a constant world of change means that your organization can keep calm and carry on amidst the chaos.

Having infrastructure and technology in place to be able to anticipate and react to market conditions is essential. However, freedom comes about only when individuals in the company are liberated from a static view of business and are able to be a part of decision-making as experts in their domain of operations. Only such a structure is agile enough to work out unforeseen challenges on its own. I have worked with clients who realized that they had a static software solution and knew this was not a true Digital Transformation. They all used smartphones and read their news online, used social media, and were dependent on smart appliances to brew their coffee, but they barely understood the software on which their business depended, and had been lulled into ignoring the vast leaps and bounds in business software, hardware, and digital communications. They had monthly savings, but no freedom to plan outside of their legacy processes. Since they had come to this realization on their own, it was relatively easy to set them on a path of total Digital Transformation, with the freedom to embrace new strategies for growth and competitiveness.

Digital Strategy Drives Digital Maturity

Organizations who embrace Digital Transformation and walk on its path reach a point at which, individually and collectively, the members attain digital maturity.

> *"Digital strategy drives digital maturity. Only 15% of respondents from companies at the early stages of what we call digital maturity — an organization where digital has transformed processes, talent engagement, and business models — say that their organizations have a clear and coherent digital strategy. Among the digitally maturing, more than 80% do."* [3]

So how do businesses focus their digital strategy effectively on creating digital maturity?

1. Capacity for Complete Transformation: The decisively differentiating characteristic of organizations with a high level of digital maturity is the emphasis they place on their digital strategy. The overall business strategy should concentrate on the ability to change the entire business. Conversely, digitally immature businesses tend to spend more time on transforming one technology at a time. Without a comprehensive, overall strategy, Digital Transformation can become easily disjointed.

2. Personal Development: More important than having programming skills, members must be able to evaluate existing technologies quickly, identify what is lacking, and then work with vendors or internally to fill in these gaps. Digitally mature companies are innovators not only in their own industry, but in business technology as well. This means, that all members must have a degree of digital literacy, with the ability to suggest and possibly implement solutions, appropriate to their tasks. Not everyone will become experts, but everyone must be technologically literate in a wide range of skills, including software coding, database technology, frontend design, social media platforms, SEO skills, and more.

Businesses must invest in their staff to transcend their technology and mature their research and development operations. The most effective organizations understand that this investment in human capital must happen across all divisions of the business.

3. Foster a Culture of Creativity: Becoming a digitally mature organization means fostering creativity. To attract and retain the best staff, it is essential that your organization have a culture that thrives on and embraces creativity. A fine example of this is Google.

Google has consistently focused their business strategy and structure on delivering software projects on the cutting edge of technology. They thrive on setting up an organizational culture that fosters creativity. This strategy has allowed them to retain the best staff and attract the best people to work for them, from all over the world. It is an extremely effective way to maintain and grow competitive advantage for an organization.

4. Create a Digital Strategy Team: At the head of your organization, there must be a digital strategy team. Without a coherent structure that includes all relevant factions of a business, there is no way any digital strategy can be successful. The team must cover all areas of business and create ways for the strategy to filter down and be embraced by all departments. A digital strategy team ensures that everybody in the organization is on the same page when it comes to driving digital change.

5. The Myth of Risk: To talk about the risk of digital technology for business is akin to talking about the risk of water overdose for a fish. Digital technology is now so well developed that it does not carry any inherent risk. It is reliable and predictable within tolerances, understood well by millions of experts around the globe, and has already penetrated into the consciousness of business. The real obstacle is psychological: the fear of not understanding Digital Transformation. Digitally mature organizations are more comfortable with taking risks. Their digital strategy is created around change.

Conversely, digitally immature organizations are a lot more risk averse and not prepared to upset the apple cart. Being risk-averse means, you are unlikely to implement and initiate change. Your business will always remain with the status quo. Unfortunately, this is not facilitating the space where organizational growth can occur. Business leaders must be prepared to put themselves on the edge of their comfort zone to see meaningful returns on their digital strategy.

The streaming media service Spotify is one example of an organization which has reached digital maturity. The music industry has been consistently disrupted over the last 30 years. Vinyl, CDs, MP3s, Cassettes, and more recently Apple's iTunes have all been disrupted. Spotify began in 2008 as a streaming music service with an emphasis on changing the business. They focused on a new type of music. In 2008 streaming was a new initiative. They used investment capital raised to buy over record labels.

The following year they released an Android and iOS version, pivoting their business to focus on the surge of popularity for smartphones. Spotify continued to focus on the skills they would need to deliver their strategy. They began talks with Facebook to integrate their platform and began investing in the right people to continue and grow music label negotiations. By 2011, they now had one million paying subscribers.

By embracing a culture of creativity, Spotify was able to continue to transform their product and maintain a high level of digital change. They even tinkered with their logo, and by 2013 they had more than 20 million users.

The digital strategy team began partnering with other companies to expand their products. Partnerships were created with Uber, Sony PlayStation, and various

US universities offering discounts for people utilizing these existing companies to subscribe to Spotify streaming.

By 2015, Spotify had disrupted the previous iron grip others had over music. They forced Apple to change their own traditional pay-per-song model and instead release Apple Music, to compete with Spotify, in 2015.

Spotify continues to take risks and lead the way in how consumers stream and digest music. In 2018, they are now arguably the leading platform in the world for consuming and streaming music. Their digital strategy drove them towards digital maturity and has allowed them to maintain their competitive advantage.

The new challenge for Spotify now is to continue to invest in research and development and adjust their digital strategy to stay at the forefront of the music business. As history shows, it is an industry that has been continually disrupted.

Business strategy must now go beyond technology to achieve effective Digital Transformation. Executives must lead the way toward an enterprise-wide strategy of empowerment, in which digital technology becomes part of all aspects of operations, and digital technology skills are part of the process of innovation.
The culture of Digital Transformation must be one of permanent transformation. This transformation must encompass not merely and not even mainly technology and the development of new technologies, but also focus on business transformation and business processes. It is important to understand the central role that organizational culture now plays in the effective execution of digital change. The challenge is developing these skills internally throughout the organization. The response to this challenge requires careful consideration of where the business wants to head

and how it will get there. The buy-in from employees across the business must be universal for Digital Transformation strategies to become successful. The more familiar a business becomes with change, the easier they are able to adapt moving forward.

Understanding that technology is no longer the main catalyst for change, instead, it is just one of the drivers of change, business leaders must also adopt a positive mindset and embrace volatility and change. Risk-taking becomes almost second nature for digitally mature organizations. They see taking risks as an excellent opportunity to drive and extend competitive advantage over their competition.

AWARENESS

Chapter Three:
The Dx Culture Code

Do not 'Go Digital,' 'Be Digital.'

A Language All Its Own

Over the last decade, Digital Transformation has become critical to business strategy in every industry. To remain agile, businesses must harness Digital Transformation effectively. The effectiveness of Digital Transformation requires several conditions. One of these is a sufficiently robust culture. Culture means the set of attitudes and practices determining how an organization responds to new information. An organization open to change has a greater chance of survival than one which resists change. It is to be contrasted to the technological level of an organization. An organization encountering new technology, even with large sums of capital at its disposal, must already have a culture embracing Digital Transformation, in order for the transformation to occur. Culture reflects one aspect of the human capital of an organization and is independent of any specific technology. When considered in terms of qualitative measurements, an organization which seeks out transformation has a culture with a relatively high capacity for change.

Any culture that is prepared to assimilate new technology effectively has a set of characteristics which I call the Dx Culture Code. However, herein lies the key dilemma: an organization having the Dx Culture Code has developed this culture through the experience of a Digital Transformation. Nevertheless, no transformation is possible without first having the Dx Culture Code.

Successful organizations break this dilemma through trial and error. I wrote this book to help organizations break this dilemma quickly. The key to breaking this dilemma is awareness. An organization must become aware of how cultural changes occur. No culture exists in a vacuum: it has developed as a set of responses to small changes over time. Yet, just as with any of us, we are better prepared for change when we are aware of how we respond to change. While changes in technology may be as obvious as the release of the desktop computer, changes in the culture of a business are more subtle. They depend on one's awareness of how members within an organization interact to, formulate and then reach corporate goals.

The Dx Culture Code builds awareness of how these changes take place within an organization. Since culture is possessed and driven by individuals and groups, organizational culture must focus on how people within an organization can have a successful impact on organizational processes and systems. The Dx Culture Code transforms corporate culture using awareness of sensitivity to change among the members of an organization to instigate Digital Transformation as a cornerstone of business strategy.

The Confluence of Digital Transformation and Organizational Culture

When we talk about Dx, I can't help but think about a client in the transportation industry that came highly recommended to me. I helped them with a small project, interfacing their work from a home- grown system into their ERP system.

The impressive thing about this company was that they had a strategy. The strategy was not to resist change and complain behind the consultants' backs while they actually held on to all the old processes.

The strategy was to use technology and be ahead of the competition constantly. They had an app allowing truck drivers to record and track time long before electronic logs were mandated by the DOT. They had a systematic model for their truck operations, and they even ran their own brokerage before anyone in the transportation industry knew anything about being efficient in keeping truck drivers home on weekends.

They are now looking into the future of investing in trucks that can drive themselves, such as those that Tesla just introduced.

I am sure this firm will continue to revolutionize their industry long before their competition even realizes that they need to do something. This firm had awareness.

Awareness is where everything begins. That's because once awareness has been established, it is possible to begin breaking the dilemma. In the Dx Culture Code, the Digital Transformation of an organization occurs within its corporate culture.

Digital Transformation began its revolution at the end of the 20th century when businesses and organizations started to go paperless and store their records electronically. Yet, within a mere twenty years, the possibilities for Digital Transformation have already entered almost every aspect of our activities and experiences.

Today, Digital Transformation stands for a multi-faceted approach that uses different elements of technology to develop new techniques and initiatives to change the way businesses operate. Information Technology has become now a catalyst for competitive advantage. Its relevance in corporate culture is well documented.

Analyzing the semantic range of our notions of *'organization'* and *'culture'* is the first step in gaining insight into why Digital Transformation necessitates their coordinated co-operation for a productive business environment to develop.

When we speak of an *"organization,"* we associate with this term a range of different associations and connotations. Specifically, we define an organization as a group of people that work together according to a set of rules and in pursuit of a particular purpose. Most organizations build up a management structure that designs and defines the relationships that are effective in coordinating the interplay between the members of the organization and their actions. This could mean a for-profit or non-profit organization, domestic or international.

Similarly, the word *"culture"* carries different connotations:

- **Community Culture:** The arts and manifestations of human intellectual achievement regarded collectively, developed in our everyday lives.

- **Organizational Culture:** A system of assumptions, values, and beliefs that are shared by those constituting an organization. These principles define the behavior of the group collectively and have an effect on how the members and participants in an organization communicate, act, and relate with others, both internally and externally.

- **Corporate Identity:** The image of itself that an organization wishes to present externally to the public. It influences and to some extent defines how consumers, shareholders, investors, and stakeholders view an organization.

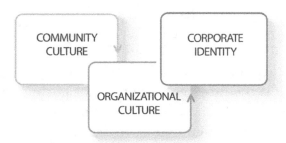

Each one of these definitions and connotations relies on human capital. Whether we are talking about an organization, a culture, or organizational culture, it is the people involved that create a collective identity.

The natural progression from this point in time onward is defining how the organizational culture and those making it work fit in with Digital Transformation. A great place to start is with the modern interdependencies of organizational culture and Digital Transformation.

Four main aspects of Digital Transformation clearly intersect with organizational culture:

1. Digital Transformation and Staff Motivation

Our definitions above show that a successful corporate culture revolves around managing people. The most critical confluence of corporate culture and Digital Transformation is that they can only work effectively if they rely on people within the organization. Ultimately, staffs are responsible for implementing technologies and strategies that bring about change. In effect, it is the strategy implemented by those working within an organization that drives the technological changes, and not the other way around.

The rise of digital change has coincided dramatically with a change in workplace culture. Modern workplaces rely on flexibility, work- life balance, and enjoyment. A lot of millennial workers, born after 1980, value income just as much as workplace satisfaction. This shift in the workplace model is reflected in Digital Transformation. Modern businesses that operate online and in a global environment are now expected to be accessible all the time.

There is no such thing as shutting down at the end of the workday anymore. Motivating staff is a key element of successful Digital Transformation and of an effective corporate culture as well. Organizations that can balance the two successfully will foster a healthy work environment. They also gain a competitive advantage that is sustainable.

Google is a great example of a company that has a very high job satisfaction rate. A major part of this satisfaction comes from the personal empowerment that Google offer their staff. Providing staff with flexibility in working space and working hours empowers staff to make their own decisions. In turn, this provides staff with a high level of intrinsic motivation, as they feel directly responsible for their own careers. It is a great way for staff to find meaning in their work.

"The company is flexible. If you're lucky, you won't have a micromanager boss, and you can be somewhat flexible in how you work. But don't get me wrong – you'll work a lot. But you don't have to do all of it chained to your desk." [4]

Google encourages an open workplace environment. It has been a courageous decision by business leaders to implement this type of strategy as it breaks away from convention and cultural norms.

However, the benefits from empowering your staff have far outweighed any potential negatives and Google has remained at the cutting edge of technology for a long period of time, so the proof is there for all to see.

2. Technology Improving Customer Experience

A major shift towards using digital technology to enhance customer experience has taken place. At the core, the culture and people within an organization are using technology to improve the business experience of those who are outside the organization, and to whom the organization is catering, the organization's customers. IT staff now have a crucial role to play in Digital Transformation. Traditionally, IT staff have already been recognized as being problem solvers. Now, however, they have become vehicles of change within an organization.

Modern corporate culture encourages IT staff to integrate technology in order to improve and enhance the business experience for both internal users and end users. Digital Transformation includes finding better ways for businesses to deliver their products/services through technology. Business strategy now involves actively investing in SMACIT (Social, Mobile, Analytical, Cloud and Internet of Things) technologies to harness a competitive advantage.

One large aspect of corporate culture consists in the way an organization communicates with its customers. Utilizing SMACIT technologies can catapult the whole online experience for customers to a new level. Businesses are able to use technology as a means to improve this experience and appeal to target customers with even more success.

3. Technology Improving the Product or Service

Modern corporate culture incorporates technology as a method to improve the product and/or service businesses are offering. This form of Digital Transformation is one example of how technology can disrupt an entire industry. However, improving a product or service through technology is intimately related to the customer and his or her experience of business. Customers realize quickly that a business' efforts to improve its products/services have immediate repercussions on the lives of the customers. They want to buy such products or services that are better than the previous options they had.

A fantastic example of an organization that is utilizing technology to improve their product is General Electric. General Electric began this process by pushing towards a culture of sustainability internally in its organizational culture. The human resources department made a concerted effort to integrate sustainability into its culture.5 Using various methodologies of well-being programs and sustainability initiatives General Electric achieved universal buy-in.

The impact of this cultural shift was that the people within the organization were now in a position to push sustainability into their products, by utilizing technology. Staff now had the skills and more importantly, the organizational backing, to make decisions and use strategies to enhance the sustainability of their products through technological advancements. This had a snowball effect and furthered the skills of many frontline staff, as well as furthering the technological advancements, in sustainability, that the company was making.

4.   Digital Transformation Improving Business Processes

Business efficiency is a very important aspect of business strategy. How well businesses manage their internal process is a central part of an organization's culture. Effective processes allow room for innovation, growth, and staff empowerment, which can, all in their own right, constitute a source of competitive advantage for a business.

Technology can be used to improve internal processes. This type of Digital Transformation is what allows businesses to become agile, adaptable, and disruptive to their industry. Digital Transformation requires a high level of innovation. However, although innovation is often associated with a level of freedom and liberty, it does require structured technological processes behind the scenes to really foster innovation.

The Dx Culture Code – How Culture Drives Digital Transformation

Being disruptive means being ahead of your competition or being where there's no competition at all. It means making it so that no one can reach your level of delivery, services, or products.

A few years ago, I was asked to help a client with their Cash Management implementation.

I'd done this many times, so I knew what to expect. When I arrived on site, I expected to have to fight and work hard to communicate my progressive system design. I came ready for battle, armed with enough PowerPoints to prove a point and explain the importance of an innovative, digital, progressive system.

To my surprise, I discovered that I did not need to convince anyone of my progressive view. The management team already had adopted a Digital Transformation culture and was leading the path of technological advancement.

They had a vision of where they wanted to go, they just didn't know how to get there. They needed guidance and a clear path in order to achieve their goal.

I remember sitting in my office, thinking how remarkable it was that in a traditional industry like the one this firm worked in, that I had landed such a forward-thinking client.

After a moment of clarity, it became clear to me: this client was unique. They had already reached the digital maturity stage.

The Dx Culture Code aims at bringing an organization to the stage of digital maturity through incremental cultural changes that continually push an organization forward with digital improvements.

It is significant that how this Dx Culture Code develops is determined by how business leaders develop their decision-making strategies. The role of business leaders in this process is becoming more and more vital. Business leaders are now beginning to incorporate Digital Transformation strategies into their main strategy conversations. A major part of Digital Transformation is that it necessitates courageous leadership. The modern business now places a real focus on people, processes, and systems within organizational decision-making.

An organizational focus on innovation will empower businesses to become adaptable. However, business leaders must make decisions that allow and trust staff to adapt to change as well. Rigidity in business decisions will be reflected in obtaining a mediocre organizational culture, and it will become a barrier for innovation. Conversely, flexibility in business strategy will be rewarded. To be flexible in strategy requires courage from the top.

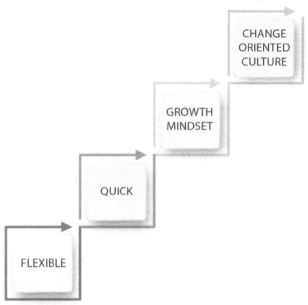

Business leaders must adopt the following attitudes and mindset for their organization to develop successfully.

- **Flexible:** A successful corporate culture must be flexible. It relies on its people to operate effectively. Similarly, Digital Transformation trusts that a business can handle adapting to change. The more flexible an organizational culture is, the easier it becomes to manage change and drive Digital Transformation forward.

- **Quick:** Digital Transformation is reflected in the speed with which an organization can produce new or disruptive technology. Similarly, if an organizational culture is quick, it allows the business to promptly place itself into a position that allows it to take advantage of any opportunity that arises.

- **Growth Mindset:** A successful corporate culture embraces the chance to grow and improve. This blends in well with Digital Transformation, which is always looking ahead for ways to initiate change.

- **Change Oriented Culture:** Corporate culture is very fluid. It is malleable depending on people and the business environment. Similarly, Digital Transformation is fluid. Technologies continue to evolve, and businesses must continue to innovate to remain competitive. Change becomes the only constant. A culture that is familiar with change has the blue print for success.

The Digital Ecosystem – Taking an Enterprise-Wide Approach to Digital Transformation

To see why Digital Transformation has to be enterprise-wide, let's travel back a few years for a trip to Kentucky.

The firm I was called in to help, was in power generation, and they had a problem: despite billions in revenue every month, it was in debt.

How had this happened?

When I arrived, I saw chaos everywhere. The left hand barely knew the right hand existed. The technology was ancient, and all of the financials – literally all of them – were being run from Excel spreadsheets.

This firm was run by a team that started together right after high school. They had all worked together for 40-50 years, and now they were all ready to retire at the same time. All of the corporate knowledge was about to walk out the door, and no new ideas were being circulated.

I saw immediately that these problems were older than most Kentucky bourbons.

It turns out that for 28 years, they had been amortizing and recording the incorrect interest on some instruments. 28 years!

I remember sitting with the Treasury Manager while she was looking at her Excel documents and comparing the numbers with my new system. The numbers were off. After a laborious verification process, she concluded that my system was right on the money. *"But how can the Excel be wrong?!"* She asked.

Together my team instituted not only a new treasury system, but also developed system controls and documentation. After we were finished, the management team was able to hire a new team, train them, and then retire. The CFO was able to refinance their debt, and with system controls in place, today they save $26 million a month all because we took a holistic view of the problem. If we had stopped fixing the Excel sheets, the organization would have failed in a matter of years. Due to their commitment to systemic transformation, today that company thrives.

Business leaders are now identifying the importance of utilizing Information Technology and their staff as a source of competitive advantage. Digital Transformation, if managed correctly, can propel businesses ahead of the competition. It is important that we examine how businesses can use Digital Transformation strategies and leverage people, and their skills, within their organization to their advantage.

Leaders are beginning to understand the importance of focusing on the digital ecosystem and the need to examine how taking an enterprise-wide approach to Digital Transformation can be beneficial to their organization.

> *"A digital ecosystem is a distributed, adaptive, open, socio-technical system with properties of self-organization, scalability, and sustainability inspired from natural ecosystems."* [6]

By breaking this definition down, we can see how each element of self- organization, scalability, and sustainability can be harnessed effectively to implement Digital Transformation and move an organization towards a position of digital maturity. As businesses shift towards digital maturity, they are able to create a sustained competitive advantage over their rivals.

The modern digital ecosystem necessitates that organizations take an enterprise-wide approach to Digital Transformation. This means that businesses must incorporate and develop digital decision-making strategies with a broad view towards how they will affect all stakeholders within an organization.

What does this look like? Taking it deeper we look at how an organization can utilize self-organization, scalability, and sustainability in their use of digital strategies to move towards a position of digital maturity.

Self-Organization

Self-Organization helps to create a successful shift towards a Dx Culture. It involves putting in place methodologies to achieve buy-in from all key stakeholders as early as possible in the timeline. How does this self-organization look when you are trying to create a Digital Transformation strategy?

- What do the customers want? Accrue information from your most important stakeholder so you can pinpoint what technologies in your organization can benefit from digital advancements.

- The organizational leadership group must organize and mobilize support for the implementation of digital projects for financial managers. Early buy-in from financial stakeholders is crucial as it ensures that everyone is on the same page and that there is no margin for miscommunications or unexpected budget blowouts.

- Each team within an organization that is involved in Digital Transformation projects must have a *'transformation leader'* or *'catalyst agent.'* This type of self-organization ensures that there are open communication lines in the organization. It helps all teams understand the interests of broader stakeholders and creates an enterprise-wide approach.

- All key stakeholders must agree on deliverables. Again, this relies on clear and specific communication channels that push forward how an organization wants to develop their technology.

In the case of the Kentucky firm, we were able to automate the HR system, so employees were able to view their vacation online, payroll data, and so on. We even went on to create notifications that gave management important information on daily operations, maintenance, and financial/accounting activities.

Scalability

Digital Transformation involves the implementation of new technologies. It is well known that new technologies require some tolerance for error from their users in the initial phases of implementation. Thus, it is extremely important that all stakeholders are considered when it comes to implementing new technologies. For scalability to be successful, all stakeholders must be on the same page. There must be agreement and understanding of the impact new technologies will have on each sector of an organization.

A series of checks and balances must be put in place across the organization and for all key stakeholders. This will help ensure that the digital progress undertakes consistent quality checks to ensure the likelihood of success. The enterprise-wide approach is so important because it gives a level of objectivity to any digital initiative.

Moreover, when one aims at making digital progress, it is important that all stakeholders learn from any digital change(s) to keep an organization moving forward. This means that for any future digital changes that are implemented and encouraged, there will be organizational-wide knowledge and experience of what can be improved and perfected.

Sustainability

Sustainability in the Kentucky example meant creating long-term, repeatable processes that would give the employees the tools to self-service within their organization. That meant creating repeatable processes, strict business rules and GAAP compliant systems. It also meant new training documentation for new employees, so that all the key processes were documented and well organized.

Sustainability in Digital Transformation is all about long-term thinking. Strategies must be created with a broad approach, but also with an approach that takes into view long-term impact and possibilities. Long-term strategies help deliver goals for all stakeholders.

- Completing digital projects well the first time saves time and money, which benefits all stakeholders equally.

- A long-term vision helps minimize mistakes and also helps with positively developing organizational culture both internally and externally, as all key stakeholders are able to see the larger picture.

- Sustainability involves an element of testing digital advancements. It creates a feedback loop which allows any bugs, errors, or fixes to be identified early on before any problems turn into major technological problems. This feedback loop helps open up communication channels across groups within an organization and also with key stakeholders.

- Long-term enterprise-wide digital strategies ensure that short- term gains are not compromised for the long-term success, but also that short-term gains do not compromise the long-term success. This creates a culture of being prepared to lose a battle or two in order to win the war.

One can identify three defining aspects of corporate culture: 1.) people working and participating in an organization 2.) the processes an organization employs, and 3.) the technology an organization uses. Yet, how they interact together decisively determines how an organization will handle Digital Transformation. Technology must now be at the forefront of every organizational decision. It can no longer be treated in isolation if businesses want to remain competitive.

The role of people within an organization has become more crucial than ever before. When understood and utilized correctly and appropriately, the Dx Culture Code helps leaders see a large lift in the value of their staff with the ability to implement digital change more effectively. The fact that this is indeed the case is reflected in the salaries that are now commanded by top IT staff as well as by the consistent demand on the labor market, particularly in the Western World, for software developers, testers, and engineers. These are the employees and workers in an organization who have become the change agents that can transform an industry.

However, Digital Transformation is so much more than simply the assembly of an organization's IT staff. It is now a key part of their business strategy. Business leaders are recognizing the importance of linking digital strategies into overall strategies. Furthermore, team leaders from every department in an organization are now becoming involved in these decision-making processes. Businesses see a deliberate shift towards including digital elements in all aspects of organizational culture.

Furthermore, we see that organizations take an enterprise-wide approach to Digital Transformation. Up-to-date organizations are prepared to involve all key stakeholders in the decision-making process. Taking on board how key interest groups will respond and integrate with digital changes and the move towards digital maturity have a strong and major influence on organizational behavior.

The underlying and unifying theme of the Dx Culture Code, however, is the confluence of Digital Transformation and organizational culture. It is clearly recognizable that organizational culture is absolutely crucial in driving technological changes within an organization.

In order to see this, we only have to look at how Google and General Electric use organizational culture to implement and drive their Digital Transformation. As a result, these organizations have reached a level of digital maturity, for which other organizations are still striving. If they wish to be disruptors instead of being disrupted by their competition, organizations must continue to strive to push their technological advancements forward. Any complacency or stagnation in Digital Transformation will result in their competition gaining the competitive advantage.

An organization's organizational culture remains the key to driving Digital Transformation that matters.

So far, I have discussed what is digital transformation and the drivers of digital transformation, but in order to effectively implement a Digital Transformation, you and the organization must be ready to embark on the digital journey. If you are a CEO, CIO, COO, CFO, CHRO or executive leader in your organization and you are reading this book right now, you need to ask yourself, do you have the leaders in place to deal with the cultural changes to provide the most benefit and the least negative impact on your organization?

Do you have a clear vision of what your digital culture stands for? What do you as an organization believe in?
If you are unclear on these answers, this indicates that you may need someone that can help you evolve into these critical factors that will be impacting your business to come.

If you do have the leadership in place, you are ready to embark on a digital journey and develop your leadership team to become a digital leader; please continue reading. If however, you are beginning to realize that there are cracks in the core foundation of your organization know that this is why I wrote this book. There is an opportunity for you to excel greatly and move forward into the opportunities that await you. However, to do this, you must realize that having a conversation with an industry leader, such as myself, to help you embrace these tactics may be needed.

You cannot embark into a Digital Journey unless everyone in your organization is ready. Every journey should start with a Discovery/Readiness Assessment. If you are talking with a consulting firm and they jump directly into solutioning without assessing the readiness of your team, you should be cautious. As an example, if my team was engaged by your company to create a digital transformation blueprint it would take an average of six weeks. If you have a complex company structure, this process may take several months.

1. Kickoff: Our team will conduct preliminary preparation calls to assess the scope of transformation potentially needed. We will send pre-meeting questionnaires to be completed in advance. This process may take on average one to two weeks.

2. Onsite interviews: We will align subject area experts in areas to be transformed. We will meet with the leadership team to understand the vision and digital direction. We will assess the level of readiness. Our subject matter experts will meet with subject matter experts of the areas of scope for our engagement. If we transform the entire organization, we will need to interview all pillars. This process will take on average two weeks. (Note: for Enterprise level clients this may take up to 3 months).

3. Report development: We will develop the report and may have follow-up questions for clarification. This process will take on average One week.

4. Story Boarding: Report delivered and reviewed – We present the story to the various business units, and the comprehensive report will provide to the management team. This process will take one week.

Note: Discovery/Readiness Assessment Blueprint is only one step in our proprietary comprehensive Digital Journey Methodology. Keep reading further on how Digital Transformation will impact your business, your growth, and your future. I encourage you to see me as your guide, mentor and leader to help you implement these ideas with great success.

AWARENESS

Chapter Four:

The Journey Towards Digital Maturity

"Though the road's been rocky, it sure feels good to me."
Bob Marley

Growing Up

The journey towards digital maturity involves a process of embracing digitalization. Modern organizations are realizing that digitalization is the new cultural norm. There has been a very apparent shift in this direction, and it is affecting every single industry. Even government departments across the world, who are usually the last to embrace change, are seeing the benefits and necessity of shifting all of their organizational processes and strategy towards digitalization.

When they say, the *"customer is king,"* it's true. The customers decide where an industry should go. It is now common place for patients around the country to being able to sign into their portal, view the results of their medical tests, communicate with their physician, and study their options online. This is the new norm. Doctors' offices that do not have this system in place may lose patients.

The journey an organization goes through to reach digital maturity is simply fascinating. It begins at the end, every business strives to reach: the end user. Consumers desire and drive the need for organizations to become digital. Consumers behavior has developed to expect and demand a noticeable level of digital capability from their vendors and suppliers when they are making product and service purchases. This shift in expectation towards digitalization as a cultural norm affects every organization and every industry in some capacity.

This expectation of digitalization is driving the need for organizations to create a digital strategy that becomes part of their corporate culture ... part of their DNA. A mature digital strategy will help set an organization onto the path of success, irrespective of the industry in which they operate. Making digitalization a part of your corporate culture can require a substantial change in organizational thinking. In most cases, it necessitates an attitudinal shift that will help your organization embrace change.

It is important to note that with Digital Transformation, digital values drive success. Success comes about if an organization utilizes and builds on key values. Digital values give the organization the ability to implement digital strategies within an evolving marketplace. Important digital values discussed in this chapter includes having a vision for change and fostering one's engagement with customers.

Organizations must embrace disruption to drive Digital Transformation effectively. Moreover, it is important to understand that disruption can occur both internally and externally within an organization. Success is often determined by an organization's ability and willingness to embrace and move towards volatility. This is because technology is an increasingly mobile space. Organizations need to become comfortable with working and developing their products and services in a rapidly changing environment.

Digitalization – The New Cultural Norm

Consumers and their expectations are largely responsible for driving the era of digitalization. Across the spectrum, consumers in the western world now demand a high level of digital integration when making purchase decisions pertaining to the products and services they would be willing to buy. In fact, digitalization has shifted so far, that consumers have become nearly entirely reliant on digital tools and modes of delivery to select and purchase what they wish to buy. Even a simple, minuscule problem such as a slightly slow loading time for a web page or app can have dire consequences for an organization's conversion of their leads into new customers and sales.

"Digitalization is a steep change even greater than the Internet. Exponential technology advances, greater consumer power, and increased competition mean [that] all industries face the threat of commoditization. The winners will act now and build a strategic advantage that leaves their counterparts wondering what happened." [7]

The follow-up question that leads on from this new cultural norm is how can businesses build a strategic advantage in the area of digitalization? Quite simply put, organizations that wish to gain a competitive advantage over their competition must be prepared to take risks. Taking risks means that business leaders must put everything on the line to create an organizational culture that fosters innovation, encourages change, and embraces advancing technology.

The development of digitalization as a cultural norm has had the direct effect of emboldening successful organizations to become risk takers. This has become a necessary step for organizations simply to remain relevant and appeal to an increasingly digitally literate consumer population. However, it must be stressed here that risk-taking does not mean taking reckless, hasty, or irresponsible digital decisions. Business leaders have to be responsible in their risk-taking. They can act responsibly by weighing the interests of all stakeholders in decision making and understanding the consequences, financial and otherwise, of making such decisions.

Risk-taking is more than just making one or two changes to technology streams within an organization. It involves the process of changing the entire attitude of an organization. It is a top-down decision that empowers employees of all levels to be prepared to fail, in order to achieve significant digital gains.

A fine example of a risk-taking organization that has embraced digitalization, specifically in their marketing campaign, is Oreo. To stay relevant, business leaders purposefully created a cultural shift within the organization to embrace digitalization and empower their employees throughout the entire organization to be prepared to take risks. Here is Vice President and brand leader for Oreo Janda Lukin explaining this process:

"You're absolutely right in that it's a cultural shift. It has taken some time for us to get there. It starts from the top, but it also starts from the bottom: You have to have people who are willing to push and take those risks. But at the same time, you need the support from the top to go and do that.

It's seeing our senior leaders enabling folks to go and make those kinds of choices and supporting them when things may not work out the way that they expect it and then rewarding them when things do go well. The people we're bringing in, we're encouraging them at very junior levels to take those risks, and we're creating a culture now that really values that. It has taken time, but I definitely have seen a cultural shift in my tenure here." [8]

Oreo has recognized the need to alter their marketing strategy to cater towards the digitalization of their industry and their consumers. It is this recognition and boldness from business leaders that has helped them maintain their position of market strength.

Make Digital a Part of Your Corporate Culture DNA

My friend Greg invested in a manufacturing firm. He asked me to come in and observe the operations with him.

He knew he had to make changes but didn't yet know exactly what. When I walked into the manufacturing facility where the firm produced their hats and coats, and custom clothing, everything was in disarray.

The cutting instruments were on a standalone table away from the fabric. In order to cut the fabric, you had to walk to the other side of the table, pick up the scissors and walk back. Once you were finished you had to walk back to return the scissors.

How inefficient!

And inefficiencies like this were everywhere. Employees had to walk back and forth all the time, wasting 3 to 4 hours a day. Greg and I observed for a while. I put together a proposal to rearrange the equipment, add additional tables, and clean up the facility.

We also sent out a questionnaire, and we found out that workers were complaining of the same things. They felt unproductive. They were tired of all the walking and felt that there should be more automation.

After six months of planning, we were ready to implement our changes. We closed the facility for three days on a weekend so that we could install new computers with large screens, rearrange the cutters, and just generally spruce up the place. We even delivered new ergonomic chairs so that everyone would be comfortable.

Would you believe that production increased by 72%?

And it kept going. We instituted a process where employees submitted recommendations weekly on improvements. Greg's investment paid off. He recuperated his money in a year, and now he has a profitable company.

We could make all these changes because we listened, and then did the hard work of changing the parts of the culture that were holding the company back.

Corporate culture is a system of assumptions, values, and beliefs that are shared by the people that make up an organization. Most importantly, these are the principles that define the behavior of the group collectively.

They have an effect on how people in an organization communicate, act, and relate with other people both internally and externally. How do these behaviors and principles become part of corporate culture DNA? The principles create ingrained values.

Thinking back to the meeting at Booz-Allen that I mentioned at the beginning of the book, it was clear to everyone in the room that the company values were ingrained into who we were: Unflinching courage, Passionate service, Ferocious integrity, Collective ingenuity, Champion's heart.

These values drove the behavior of the organization, and it drove all of us to be at our best.

Corporate culture DNA is to incorporate being digital as an effective element of your corporate culture. This can be a difficult task, but it is not an impossible one. To develop your organization to a level of digital maturity, I have created a framework you can follow, irrespective of the industry or business sector within which you operate.

Making digital a part of your corporate culture DNA allows your business to become more flexible and respond appropriately to changes that occur with Digital Transformation.

1.   Developing a Well-defined Strategic Path

The most important step an organization can take to make digital a part of their corporate culture is creating a clear, unambiguous strategic path for employees and leaders to follow. This process involves creating **SMART** goals that outline how you can use digitalization to transform your business. After all, it is the strategy that defines the technology that helps businesses take advantage of digital opportunities.

- **Specific:** Create goals that have a high level of specificity around digital performance. How can technology aid your value proposition? How can technology help your marketing campaign so that you can deliver your message to your target market? What digital advancements can you make to improve your conversion rates? How can you use digitalization effectively to draw in new customers?

- **Measurable:** The goals must also be measurable. To make digitalization a part of your organization's culture, the steps you take must have parameters put around them. What are the analytics you are going to put around digital implementation? How will you measure success? Without measuring performance, it is impossible to provide feedback to relevant teams so that they can make improvements and progress.

- **Achievable:** The goals need to be achievable, but they must also set down a challenge for an organization. Going digital requires a transformational change. Your goals should realize and identify where changes need to be carried out within an organization. Your goals should also challenge your team to carry them through.

- **Realistic:** Digital goals must be realistic. If your industry is slow in adapting to digital change, then creating a culture that embraces digitalization must be initiated incrementally. This process involves uncovering what digital expectations are in your marketplace and striving to surpass those expectations without stretching your business too far.

- **Time-Framed:** Digital goals must also be measured over a specific period to be successful. Having a measured length of time gives your business team time to adapt to change and push your organizational culture towards embracing Digital Transformation.

2. Understand Where Your Business Fits within the Digital Landscape

To make digitalization a part of your corporate culture DNA, you have to truly understand where your business fits in the digital landscape. This begins with knowing your target market. When you understand your end users intricately, you can begin to implement digital technologies that cater towards their needs. Without this market research, there is no way of knowing if your digital initiatives are going to be successful. When trying to make digitalization an integral part of your culture, it is critical that your business has early success. This gives your team confidence in the system and provides an openness to change. Set up your business to have early wins with proven digital methods to drive this digital change from within.

It is not enough to know your end user. You must also know your competitors. It is essential to understand what digital processes they are using and identify the opportunities and threats associated with them. This allows your business to find areas to grow market share and build team trust in your digital strategy.

3. Know Your USP (Unique Selling Point)

Whether you are a business that provides products or services, you must know your unique selling point. Understanding your point of difference in the marketplace allows you to focus your attention on developing digital technologies that cater towards this. It is likely your business team already understands your USP well if your business is successful. Creating digital technologies that integrate well with your USP is playing to your strengths. It gives you a clear strategic direction for your organization and a clear path for your staff to follow. Focusing on strengths will foster the embrace of digital changes and push your corporate culture towards a more mature digital model.

4. Move Towards Integration

No matter where your business sits on the business spectrum, it is important that you move your digital strategy towards integration. What does this mean? First, it involves identifying which digital channels you currently utilize that convert into paying customers.

Once you have a clear understanding of what converts, you can integrate your content across the digital channels that you use. Once you have integration across digital channels, it is important that you create open communication streams across business sectors.

This allows your teams to work together to enhance your digital footprint and success. It is also another step towards creating a successful digital culture. Finally, it is important that these integrations are measured. Understanding how each digital implementation performs will help your team identify the areas accurately in order to pursue and bring in more paying customers.

5. Up-skill Your Digital Staff

To make digitalization a part of your corporate culture DNA, it is absolutely essential to give your employees the right tools to grow the digital skills of the company. Giving the opportunity for staff to up-skill is a necessary research and development cost that will save your business time and money in the long run.

Internal up-skilling has the added benefit of being able to grow your digital capacity with staff that already have valuable, inside company knowledge and information. They already know how the business works. Thus, they will be able to tailor their digital skills effectively for the benefit of the organization.

6. Promote a Flexible Business Environment

Promoting a flexible business environment must begin at the top with business leaders. Business leaders have to change their attitudes to encourage digital innovation. Small and medium-sized organizations are often discouraged, because of the high costs frequently associated with research and development. However, businesses must try and look past the initial costs of research and development and focus on the long-term benefits of creating flexibility.

So, how do business leaders create flexibility? They must encourage and empower their digital team with open, collaborative processes to improve existing technologies and try new technologies. It requires a certain level of boldness and a willingness to accept that there will be failures along the way. Accepting these failures as learning and not discouraging team members go a long way in creating a corporate culture that embraces digital behaviors.

7. Apply Analytics Effectively

When you are trying to create a digital organizational culture, analytics are a key tool to measure growth and success. Nearly all businesses measure analytics in some form or another. However, it is how you utilize these analytics that makes all the difference.

To encourage digital growth, business leaders must make a concerted effort to review analytics and consider how effectively they manage strategic goals. Consistent review allows business departments to make informed decisions on where to make changes and where to continue to push for growth. Accurate and effective analytics allows your digital teams to strive for improvement and make progress across the organization.

8. Encourage Internal Digital Transformations

It is important here to note the value of internal Digital Transformation. Internal customers, staff, and people connected to an organization have the added benefit of having inside knowledge. They understand the workings and mechanics of an organization extremely well. As a result, this knowledge can be transferred into the use of digital technologies to make gains in efficiency and effectiveness as they relate to running an organization.

Furthermore, internal digitalization is fantastic for spreading by word of mouth and for the cultural success of an organization. People will quickly catch on if an organization is a great place to work when they are utilizing new technologies and encouraging employee empowerment to develop digital maturity.

How Digital Values Drive Success

The road to digital maturity is paved by organizations having the ability to innovate continuously. However, continuous innovation requires organizations to have strong digital values to drive them towards digital maturity. Strong digital values allow organizations to react, adapt, and remain agile in a fast-paced environment.

So, what are the key digital values and how do they drive success?

KEY DIGITAL VALUES THAT DRIVE SUCCESS

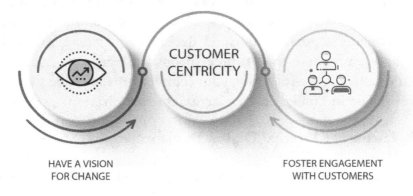

CUSTOMER CENTRICITY

HAVE A VISION
FOR CHANGE

FOSTER ENGAGEMENT
WITH CUSTOMERS

1. Have a Vision for Change

A vision for change is a core digital value that drives success. Having a vision for change is fundamental for an organization to be able to plan a business strategy effectively. A vision for change also helps an organization leverage its culture to create a future which embraces and moves toward progressive technologies. It is an empowering step for staff and business leaders alike to know that the organization is prepared to shift their strategy to improve their digital technology continually.

What does this staff empowerment look like for an organization? It results in reduced turnover, reduced recruitment costs, increased employee engagement, and makes an organization a more desirable place to work in the eyes of prospective employees. These are all important aspects of creating the right organizational culture that fosters Digital Transformation.

2 Foster Engagement with Customers

The introduction of new digital technologies should be made with the end user in mind. Before an organization commits to change, they should be certain that the changes will be beneficial for their staff and customers. Customer engagement will point an organization in the right direction for areas where improvements to digital technology can be made.

Significantly, engaging effectively with customers is a digital value that requires so much more than simply collecting data and numbers. It involves engaging with customers on a personal level to find out about their motivations and how satisfied they are with the digital experience you are offering. As soon as you understand why your customers make decisions, you can make informed decisions on how to tweak and improve your digital strategy.

Here's what I mean about digital cultural values driving success.

In 2005, the country's most famous aerospace company was looking for experts who understood cost accounting as well as various ERP systems, and I was one of the few who qualified for the job.

I was hired and found myself in charge of finance transformation initiatives across their organization. They had over 700 legal entities across the world. Seven hundred! All with varied and often conflicting corporate cultures.

To start to wrap my mind around all these different cultures – and, where needed, I knew the biggest challenge was going to be getting them to agree. This was the first company where I had to have mediators in the room while trying to agree on common chart of account elements. This firm knew that they needed to transform their cultures if they would have any hope of being successful with business transformation or Dx.

Embrace Disruption to Drive Digital Transformation – A Focus on Internal and External Disruption

Success is often determined by an organization's ability to embrace market volatility. Unfortunately, due to the rapid speed at which technology is changing, the natural reaction to volatility and change in the marketplace is to become insular and resistant to change.

Business leaders must make a conscious decision to embrace technological change and volatility. This means leaders must put in place a series of checks and balances for constant feedback when carrying out technological advancements. Being open to feedback allows changes to be made as they happen. In delivering technology based projects, teams often put blinders on to complete the project, only to find that the technology has moved on by the time they have reached completion.

Embracing volatility keeps communication channels open and allows teams to be open to digital change. In turn, this creates digital agility and can create a competitive advantage that makes a business easily adaptable.

"Disruption is not negative, but necessary. We need to ensure that we are the ones disrupting our own business for the greater good, before someone else disrupts our market and takes our customers. External forces shouldn't be the only catalyst for this shift. Rather,

new technologies and innovations should be embraced as part of a refreshed business strategy and culture shift.

Ask yourself, "Why am I implementing this application, technology, or method? How will it keep my business model and service offerings relevant to the market? How will it improve on my unique value proposition, or create a new one? Will this give me a long-term strategic benefit or is it simply a short-term fix?

If you can't pinpoint the 'why' of a disruptive technology and ensure that it aligns with the goals of your business, you are just playing catch up and likely creating greater confusion and negative disruption for your own staff and customers." [9]
- Shane Baker, CEO of TAS

Conversely, internal disruption focuses more on processes. Digital Transformation is not only about enhancing the technologies for end users; it is also about the digitalization of business processes. Embracing disruption internally means that businesses must have the ability to change and improve their procedures.

Business leaders must empower their business teams to challenge their automation, analytics, and accuracy continually. Being open to internal disruption allows businesses to become more adept to change, increase efficiency, and lower their overall costs.

On the contrary, external disruption is about how an organization uses Digital Transformation to disrupt their industry or the marketplace they operate in. This process involves utilizing technologies to provide a point of difference for your product and service. The impact is that customers become more engaged with your product/service because of technology and this helps your organization pick up more market shares. Let's look at how two organizations disrupted their marketplace.

Airbnb and Uber are great examples of market disruption. They have both used Digital Transformation to exploit the gaps in the market share of the economy. They both identified that people wanted autonomy, when it came to accommodation and transport, respectively.

They then catered their digital technologies to create an experience for their users that replicated this autonomy. Users can now get a ride in most cities in the world, or book accommodations nearly anywhere in the world, simply by using an application on their phone.

These two organizations have changed the way their industries now operate. They have effectively disrupted two major and usually well-settled markets. As a result, their competition either has to get on board, or face becoming obsolete within a very short period.

External disruption is not without its challenges. In most situations, it involves utilizing novel or unique techniques. It may take time for consumers to adjust to change and many organizations have faced initial resistance to this change. Yet remember technological advancements have only been beneficial throughout the course of history. Organizations should be encouraged to persevere. Remember, at one time, people used to think the world was flat, the earth was the center of the universe, and that there was not a lot of land beyond continental Europe and Asia.

Challenging consumer beliefs takes some courage, but it is this type of external disruption where technological advancements are beneficial for organizations and society as a whole.

Digital maturity is a process that requires a courageous mindset and an adventurous attitude from business leaders that filters throughout an organization. To be competitive in our digital age, organizations are beginning to understand that they have to be risk takers. Digitalization is the new cultural norm. In order to stand out from the crowd and develop a sustained competitive advantage, it is no longer enough to maintain the status quo. Organizations must embrace and actively seek technological advancements that can improve both their internal and external processes.

So much of the journey towards digital maturity depends on an organization's digital strategy. There is a defined, proven process on how a business can effectively create a culture so that digital strategy intrinsically becomes a part of your corporate culture DNA.

Increasingly, we are finding that organizations in all industries are affected. Digitalization is changing all industries in some way. The level at which organizations embrace this digital shift and invest in their technologies is what is determining their success. Interestingly, this shift to digital maturity involves more of a strategic, cultural, and attitudinal shift in comparison to the actual technologies themselves.

An organization utilizing key values. drive Digital Transformation. Business leaders must have a vision for change in their organization and engage effectively with their end users to cater effectively to their customers in an evolving marketplace.

Organizations must also embrace disruption to drive this Digital Transformation. Disruption can take two forms. It can be internal, in the form of digital disruption of internal processes, methodologies, and procedures. It can also be external, in the form of digital disruption that changes the behavior of consumers and how they use technology in the marketplace.

Part Two:
AWAKEN

Chapter Five:

Leading The Digital Transformation

Only leaders who master Digital Transformation will stay ahead by using digital technology to create new markets or drive efficiencies.

My friend Tim owned a rehabilitation company. He helps injured soldiers to walk again.

The process was very difficult, but he had a high success rate. One day, Tim asked me if I could come observe and help him figure out something more revolutionary. He was always looking for something unique, something no one else was doing. He also wanted to scale his operation through technology but did not know how.

I visited his facility, and after a month of observation, Tim and I got together for some brainstorming. We went through my questionnaire. We finally came up with developing a virtual reality tool that was going to take soldiers into their dream world, helping them visualize being fully healthy and walking.

After six months of development, the VR tool was ready to be put into action. This tool allowed Tim's patients to recover at previously unknown rates of success and, in turn, did the same for Tim's business.

Tim knew that Digital Transformation is all around us; it's just a matter of finding the right places to apply it.

Digital Transformation explores the changing face of technology and the impact it has on business. Specifically, the mechanics of Digital Transformation look at how new and improved information technologies can be a catalyst for creating a sustained source of competitive advantage over the competition.

Digital Transformation has progressed far beyond the traditional realms of transforming data from paper to an electronic format and into software. Technologies are now being used as a major source of innovation to disrupt traditional industries, provide new avenues to appeal to consumers, and create new sources of revenue. Because of this shift in the use of technology, the way in which Digital Transformation is carried through has become critically important.

The importance of organizational culture and the significance which leadership plays in the culture shift that empowers Digital Transformation is essential to success. Leadership must create a culture that embraces change. Organizations must examine how leaders can directly contribute to this cultural shift that will help foster Digital Transformation internally and lead to a higher level of digital ability and innovation.

The transformation has to occur from the top down and the bottom up simultaneously. Digital Transformation requires strong leadership from the top. Yet it also necessitates buy-in from the bottom up and from those staff who are working at the coalface of the industry, particularly in relation to customers. Without their support for change, ideas for Digital Transformation will not get off the ground.

In order to successfully lead the Digital Transformation, it is important to understand what is required from business-decision makers to become digitally savvy leaders so that they can become digital evangelists. Understanding the skills and proficiencies that need to be learned and developed to help an organization reach its technological potential can mean the difference between success and failure.

Digital leaders understand the importance of setting clear goals and providing the needed direction by articulating the steps that business leaders can take to set the standards within an industry and, in turn, how to use technology to stay one step ahead of the competition.

Why Leadership Is Crucial to the Culture Shift and Digital Transformation

Those who are in leadership positions within an organization are entrusted with the role of leading an organization towards a culture that encourages and fosters Digital Transformation. Increasingly, we see that it is culture, not technology that drives Digital Transformation. Business leaders carry the responsibility of driving corporate culture. They must be visible to staff and lead from the front to display that they are heavily involved in digital change:

> *"Employees in digitally maturing organizations are confident in their leaders' ability to play that digital game. More than 75% of respondents from these companies say that their leaders have sufficient skills to lead the digital strategy. Nearly 90% say their leaders understand digital trends and technologies. Only a fraction of respondents from early-stage companies have the same levels of confidence: Just 15% think their leaders possess sufficient skills, and just 27% think their leaders possess sufficient understanding."* [10]

Leadership is so crucial for driving a culture of digital empowerment because cultural change is a difficult process. It requires a considerable level of risk-taking and courage from those at the top to take an organization in a new direction. It is the responsibility of the business leaders to lead the way and be prepared to pivot the way in which an organization utilizes technology. Business leaders must make bold decisions, and strong leadership will flow through an organization. A successful Digital Transformation culture will empower staff to make decisions without the fear of failure and encourage them to use their skills to transform the technology of an organization.

Business leadership must also place a high value on internal innovation. This requires an elevated level of adaptability within an organization. In order to encourage adaptability, business leaders must show a high level of faith and trust in their employees. A linear business strategy that does not allow for employee empowerment will be reflected in the behavior of employees. However, if business leaders encourage a certain level of risk-taking and innovation in business strategy, employees will reflect this in organizational culture and demonstrate the benefits in the form of technological gains.

Leadership is crucial in recognizing the role of IT staff within an organization. It is the role of the Chief Technical Officer (CTO) to be a change agent for decision-making and innovation.

"CTOs need to take a more prominent leadership role. With an eye for providing customers or clients with top-end efficient technologies, CTOs represents a unique blending of priorities belonging to both the CMO and the CIO. The CTO plays a uniquely critical role, offering an external-facing perspective to balance the CIO's more internal focus" [11]

A high level of involvement from technology leaders within a business empowers IT staff to develop innovative projects for customers, which acts like a snowball effect to attract new customers and encourage further innovation. With Digital Transformation, the more change that is initiated within an organization, the easier it becomes to implement, as employees become more adaptable and at ease with volatility.

A great example of innovation in action is the supermarket chain TESCO. TESCO business leadership emboldened their technology team to introduce new innovations when they expanded into the South Korean market. They set a goal of increasing revenue without having to increase the number of stores they had. What resulted was a unique innovation (in 2013) that transported the store to the people. TESCO used technology in an unprecedented way – they became a food chain that created virtual grocery aisles at subway stations. Customers then could scan the items using their Smartphones for purchase. The items were then delivered when they returned home. The result was that TESCO was able to increase revenue while lowering their fixed capital costs in a new and innovative way.[12]

This innovation shows how business leadership could encourage Digital Transformation within any industry. TESCO, a supermarket chain, used mobile technology and a unique digital strategy to take advantage of something so simple as people waiting for the train to increase and expand their revenue potential. This digital innovation provided a source of competitive advantage for TESCO and encouraged them to expand their digital innovations further. A few well-calculated risks taken by leadership have helped create a cultural shift within TESCO that fosters innovation.

Transformation from Top to Bottom and from Bottom to the Top

Digital Transformation involves a two-step process to be successful within an organization. The shift in strategy must come, first, from the top down, and, secondly, also from the bottom to the top. This means that leaders must lead from the front with regard to initiating digital strategy. Furthermore, it means that there must be universal buy-in from employees on the front line for this strategy to work out well. In order to take a closer look at the requirements of this transformation, we can inspect the steps that leadership can take to create a top-down effect and how such an initialization can flow on to a bottom-up approval of digital change as well.

For Digital Transformation to be successful business leaders cannot delegate. They must be the ones demonstrating the behaviors they wish to see within an organization. Since Digital Transformation cannot be delegated, leaders must set realistic expectations.

> *"We talk a great deal about Digital Transformation. We state that it must start from the top – the executive – and filter down and across to all areas of an organization that once were comfortably siloed. We also point out that Digital Transformation represents a mindset change that must fully align the business around the customer."* [13]

A top-down strategy must include the necessary organizational structural operations, which are important for implementing change. However, more importantly, leaders must have the attitude that fits with what the organization wants to achieve. If a business wants to become innovators and industry disruptors, business leaders must be prepared to show actively that they encourage and support a level of risk-taking and the ability to change the direction of the organization. This requires sufficient flexibility in thinking. Leaders must accept that change is the only constant within an organization when making a decisive cultural shift towards Digital Transformation.

The top-down and bottom-up approaches are interdependent. One cannot be successful without the other. Organizations require strong leadership from the top to implement Digital Transformation strategies. Essentially, business leaders empower their staff. It is then in the hands of managers, employees, and line staff to give action to innovation. This is where the bottom-up strategy is important.

> *"In an ideal world, Digital Transformation should have the*

commitment of those at the top of their organizations. At the same time, it's notable that the Digital Transformation that has been taking place so far has been occurring more at the grassroots level – employees or managers putting technology in place to boost their areas of the business." [14]

Technological disruption occurs at the frontline of organizations. This is because employees have the greatest exposure to consumers. They have the necessary understanding of the needs of the customer. They can make decisions on how technology can improve the existing customer experience or attract new customers. Frontline employees also have an understanding of how customers interact with technology and have firsthand use of data and analytics to understand where gains can be made. If employees are aligned with the overall strategy, they are more likely to express their views and implement technological changes, without fear of retribution.

In reality though, organizational culture treads a fine line between innovation and chaos. If the business strategy for Digital Transformation is clear and coherent, then employees understand the parameters of the business vision and feel empowered to engage in innovation. Conversely, a top-down strategy with no structure, purpose, or attitude can cause chaos in a bottom-up approach.

Burberry, the luxury goods retailer, is a fantastic example of a firm that has successfully implemented a simultaneous top down and bottom up approach to Digital Transformation. The CEO at the time, Angela Ahrendts, created a clear digital strategy with an accompanying mindset that fostered employee innovation and change throughout the whole organization. Burberry achieved this by flipping the traditional innovation model on its head. She created two working groups one for tabling ideas and a second for turning these ideas into innovation reality. With a strong desire for innovation, Burberry created a culture where the youngest and brightest talent in the organization could dream up ideas that could be actioned within the organization. Burberry allowed junior staff to create ideas and then the second working group, made up of senior executives, would implement the best ideas. In effect, Burberry was creatively led from the bottom up because of the fluid top-down strategy that was in place. The youngest and brightest employees in the company felt empowered to innovate, and the Burberry strategy had complete buy-in throughout the whole organization.[15]

Becoming a Digitally Savvy Leader

Becoming a digitally savvy leader requires having an understanding of the technologies that can lead to disruption within an industry. More importantly, however, digitally savvy leaders must understand the mechanisms that lead to change and work closely with the people within the organization who are capable of initiating change.

> *"Technology knowledge is not the most important skill leaders need to have. In an open-ended question, respondents said that the ability to steer a company through a business model change is the most important skill, cited by 22%. Being a forward thinker is almost as important, with 20% of respondents placing it in the top spot."* [16]

How do you develop these skills and filter them down throughout the organization? We have created a list of seven capabilities a business leader must have to become digitally savvy.

1. Inspiring Leadership – Business leaders must inspire leadership in a digital context. This means that it is the responsibility of business leaders to motivate staff and grow confidence in digital technologies. This is the case particularly in industries that are slow adopters of technology. Leaders must show a propensity to see and respond to change and value opportunities that can be found in business uncertainty.

2 Competitive Mindset – Business leaders must have the capability to motivate staff to compete as industry leaders through the use of technology. It involves encouraging experimentation and having a no-fear mentality when it comes to testing and trying new initiatives.

3. Clear Strategy – It is the role of the business leader to define a clear strategic path with other decision makers and key stakeholders within an organization that set the goals of Digital Transformation.

4. Impact – Business leaders must use the influence of their position with positive impact. This means that their dialogue and actions must reflect a transformative digital philosophy. It is essential that all senior business leaders are on board with this attitude because a breakdown in communication at the top level can affect the buy-in from employees who see a lack of cohesiveness as a weakness of business strategy.

5. Collaborate – People are the key to any successful Digital Transformation. Business leaders must form relationships and constantly communicate with key employees and stakeholders, so that they remain close to the action with regard to decision making.

6. Implementation – It is the role of business leaders to utilize their position to execute the parallel development of people and technology. In other words, creating a workforce that is adaptable to changeable technologies and developing the skills of employees to meet the current needs of the business environment.

7. Succession – Business leaders must be aware that Digital Transformation is not a one-off event. To remain an industry leader, business leaders must actively pursue constant innovation and drive to recruit the best talent available to increase research and development capabilities.

If business leaders can showcase these skills, it will not take long for employees in an organization to reciprocate these behaviors. In effect, digitally savvy leaders pioneer the way in how the organization will operate. How leaders operate is often reflected in the dominating behaviors of an organization's culture.

When Leaders Become Digital Evangelists

A strong connection between rhetoric and action surrounding technological developments breeds business leaders who can become and be effective digital evangelists. Business leaders must show action that backs up their statements, supporting the importance of technology investment. A disconnect between the two has the effect of demonstrating to the rest of the organization and to key stakeholders that the leaders are not really taking Digital Transformation seriously.

> *"Surveys undertaken by global research firms often reveal a 'disconnect' between what respondents say they'll do and how they actually behave. A recent example of this was revealed when Gartner researchers asked Asia-Pacific CEOs about technology investment. While most executives maintained that technology was a chief priority, their investment in new systems did not mirror that contention."* [17]

So, what can business leaders do to ensure that they become digital evangelists? How can they then maintain this outlook?

There are three crucial steps that business leaders must take to drive an organization forward in its journey towards Digital Transformation.

1. Business leaders must propel organizational change and not just technological change – It is easy for business leaders to concentrate solely on technological advancements when trying to implement Digital Transformation. However, it is crucial that technology innovation is carried out simultaneously with organizational change. A crucial link exists between organizational culture and mindset that fosters digital innovation. This is where the actions and rhetoric of business leaders must marry up to encourage a mindset of trial and innovation.

2. Business leaders must encourage digital enthusiasm through their actions – Digital Evangelists must be prepared to drive the conversations with IT that challenge and drive the development of technology. Leaders must ask how technology can be utilized to add value to existing products or services. They must ask how technology can open up access to new markets or new revenue streams. Leaders must also be prepared to ask how the organization can develop to disrupt their industry. These conversations will open up communication channels with IT staff and strategists which have the effect of opening the door to Digital Transformation possibilities and encourage staff to put forward and carry out trials of new ideas and new ways of thinking.

3. Business leaders must revolutionize how IT is positioned to lead digital growth – It is well documented that technologies can change the way an organization operates its core business. Business leaders must position IT teams in such a way that they drive this digital growth. Business leaders must provide clear strategic goals and ambitions, and foster the right skills to build digital capability. Investing in up-skilling key staff and setting clear expectations of how IT can provide digital change provides growth opportunities for an organization. There must also be a clear and open dialogue between IT teams and other sectors of the business so that everybody is on the same page as to how technology can enhance what an organization is able to offer.

One example of business leaders executing the steps identified above and behaving like Digital Evangelists is Monsanto. Monsanto is an agriculture biotechnology firm that strives to enhance farming and agriculture methods for ecological and sustainable farming. Business leaders identified the need to utilize technology effectively to drive innovation. However, they also understood that they needed to drive that change through their actions. This was reflected in their investment strategies.

"A key turning point in Monsanto's history occurred in 2012, as we started acquiring companies producing digital tools and data modeling to provide even more precision-focused solutions for farmers. We established technology and learning centers throughout the

U.S. to help the industry understand more about the planet that feeds us. We continue to institute outreach programs with the goal of improving the lives of families and communities around the world, including in our hometown of St. Louis, Missouri." [18]

This example shows business leaders acting in a way that drove forward innovation and digital change. Their actions helped create a culture that embraced Digital Transformation. Monsanto is now positioned as a world leader that utilizes technology to drive business growth and helps with the sustainability of the planet and its natural resources at the same time.

Leading the Digital Transformation requires bold and courageous leadership. Strong leadership helps drive organizational culture. A strong organizational culture that is blended with an effective digital strategy will foster technological innovation.

Business leaders that are prepared to pioneer their organization towards digital innovation are the ones who are also prepared to back up their rhetoric with strong action. Leaders pave the way for their staff to act with freedom and create ideas that can transform into technological initiatives. A culture that is prepared to fail and challenge existing technologies is likely to be more adaptable and susceptible to change. Leaders that encourage this behavior empower staff to take responsibility for the change as well. Taking a top-down and bottom-up approach to Digital Transformation is an effective way to ensure that there is organizational consistency and coherence in delivering technological advancements.

In many instances, it is the frontline staff who are consistently engaging with customers and working on the frontline that have the best grasp of how technology can be utilized to improve how a business delivers its products or services. Business leaders must embrace this type of thinking and foster this growth, much like Burberry and TESCO have managed to do in their own unique way.

The challenge for business leaders is to ensure that this freedom and empowerment of staff is aligned with effective goals and structures so that such initiatives do not descend into chaos. While risk-taking is part of the Digital Transformation process, informed decisions should ensure that these risks are calculated too. Ultimately, business leaders are responsible for the performance and future of an organization. Therefore, they must be the ones who ensure that there is equal opportunity for technology and strategy to develop simultaneously within the fabric of an organization's culture.

AWAKEN

Chapter Six:

Drivers of Digital Transformation

Strategy is the health of all driving forces of Digital Transformation.

Digital Transformation is the process of aligning organizational strategy and culture to implement technological change. The introduction and development of new technologies is crucial in modern business to help businesses thrive in a competitive environment. Technology development is now used as an effective instrument to disrupt industries and change the way that products and services are delivered to consumers.

In the previous chapters, we have covered what it takes to lead the Digital Transformation. Now it is time to take a closer look at the drivers of Digital Transformation and the individual elements of Digital Transformation that are relevant for businesses that want to implement an effective digital strategy.

Let's evaluate these three significant drivers.

1. Competitive Threat – The threat of competition inspires and drives a lot of the need for businesses to invest in technology. Organizations see innovation, research, and development as a necessity in order to stay ahead of one's competition. Furthermore, constant innovation and investment in technologies are essential to retain an advantage over the competitors in one's industry. For the best technological developments, it does not take long for imitators to appear. This is why businesses cannot afford to be stagnant when it comes to driving Digital Transformation. Otherwise, they will simply be overtaken by their competition.

2. The Customer Experience (Cx) – Businesses are constantly trying to enhance the ways they deliver products and services to their customers. The development of technology is a fantastic method to enhance the user experience. By making incremental gains in facilitating and improving the customer journey, it is possible to expand existing consumer markets and tap into new uncharted market segments. Customers now have certain expectations when it comes to technology. They expect a proficient level of speed and service, irrespective of which industry an organization is operating in. This is simply the nature of technology in the modern business environment. Providing improvements for customers is an ideal way to become an industry disruptor, appeal to a much wider consumer base, and drive opportunities for growth.

3.   Strategic Cost Optimization – Businesses strive to lower their costs of producing technological innovations. This involves a balancing act of investing in the skills and attributes of staff and creating effective retention and recruitment strategies. When it comes to Digital Transformation, the skills of people implementing technological change are the most important asset to lowering costs. It is a classic case of the economies of scale. The more individuals within an organization become familiar with creating and producing technological innovations, the lower the cost of each successive innovation.

Streamlining and rationalizing platforms, applications, processes, and services are the fourth driver of Digital Transformation. These actions one can take rely on the integration and the coherent collection of data, accurate and frequent testing, and appropriate risk assessments that are led by business leaders. Automation is a key aspect of this driver as it allows businesses to become more efficient in their internal processes and frees up the ability of staff to put more concerted efforts into research and development.

Operational agility is the fifth and last significant driver of Digital Transformation. It focuses on the ability of businesses to adopt flexible processes that can be fitted with the overall strategy of an organization. Flexibility is crucial in allowing businesses to grow and develop in sync with technological changes and adjust the way business is carried out if necessary.

We can see all five of these drivers in the case of a large car rental company who brought me in to consult.

This firm had systems. Many, many systems.

AS400 for inventory, Oracle for financials, Workday for HR, and then every tech vendor had a software or hardware in the company. And because the company had become the behemoth it was through mergers and acquisitions; it was a technical and cultural mishmash, a Frankenstein's monster of organizational capacities.

The management team wanted to modernize the technology, but not just the technology – they understood that alongside, these cultures would need to change too. They saw that it wouldn't all transform overnight.

And so, after much preparation, we implemented the Ronin platform that sits on top of all multiple systems.

The results were astonishing. Implementation time: eight weeks. After those eight weeks, we reduced the time managers needed to manage their reservations from four hours to five minutes. You read that right: from hours to literally minutes!

We replaced the computer terminals with tablets. That made it all more portable, and because managers were now freed from printing reports and shuffling paper, they could focus on up-sale and customer satisfaction.

Revenue increased.

Even training time went from months to just a few days now that managers no longer had to be trained on eight different systems. Overnight the organization became digital without replacing all of their systems, and it revolutionized everything. The company recouped its investment in the first 12 months.

The result for the customer: The transaction times were cut in half, and satisfaction went through the roof.

1. Competitive Threat

The threat of falling behind the competition is a major reason why organizations drive their own Digital Transformation. This threat revolves around the fear of losing revenue and market share to other market players in the industry. With the advancement of technology, the market share and loyalty of customers, in particular, has become a lot more volatile.

"Competitive pressure is driving 70% of Digital Transformation projects globally, according to new research. With over a third of companies believing that failure to complete Digital Transformation projects will result in competitors taking advantage, market concerns are high when it comes to bringing internal processes and infrastructure up to date." [19]

In some respects, implementing digital strategies and rolling out technological advancements has become almost a race to win over customers first. E-commerce strategies are being created at breakneck speed to try and beat competitive pressures. However, it is also important to note that Digital Transformation is not a one-off process. Even the best organizations at the forefront of Digital Transformation need to evolve and develop new technologies continually. This is because competitors will quickly imitate and evolve for themselves the most successful technologies within an industry. If an organization becomes stagnant, other market players will quickly take their customer base.

Competitive threat, moreover, is also what has driven many digital disruptors in the first instance. Digital disruptors can be defined as organizations that have pioneered new technologies to exploit opportunities for expanding their customer base and revenue share. In the process, these organizations have successfully disrupted an entire industry.

Netflix is a great example of a digital disruptor that has utilized streaming to display online content. They have used the boom of Internet streaming to target, until now, a largely non-digitized industry. Netflix was able to use their already established customer base to stave off any potential competitors who were looking to use the same path.

Netflix based their streaming model on a need to compete in the market. They were driven to technological change by a competitive threat. What happened next is simply remarkable. Netflix has single-handedly caused the demise of video stores. Netflix now has online shows committing to being solely released on their platform. Furthermore, they have used their technology cleverly, introducing "binge- watching" by playing subsequent episodes continually. They are continually investing in technology to sustain their Digital Transformation – and even this is still driven by competitive threat.20

2.   Customer Experience

The Customer Experience is another main driver of Digital Transformation. How customers interact with your product or service can be a catalyst for driving strategy and curating technological advancements.

Five main steps need to be considered in the customer experience. These are important to how a business will drive forward Digital Transformation.

01 FIND THE OUTCOME YOUR CUSTOMERS ARE LOOKING FOR

02 DETERMINE YOUR CUSTOMER'S MINDSET

03 MAP YOUR CUSTOMER'S JOURNEY

04 KNOW CUSTOMER EXPECTATIONS

05 UNDERSTAND THE MARKETPLACE

- **Find the outcome your customers are looking for** – Any technological development or advancement must be centered on the goals of the customer. Any technological change must improve the customer experience of your product or service.

  For example, Uber improved their customer experience by creating an easy real-time taxi mobile application with electronic payments. They cater to the needs of their customers by creating an easy-to-use platform that is quick, efficient, and automated. They focused on the outcome the customer was looking for, and by delivering on customer experience, they were able to disrupt an entire industry.

Many organizations can get caught up and entangled with the fact that technological changes are made for internal reasons. At the end of the day, it is important not to lose sight of who you are serving and what you are trying to achieve for them.

- **Determine your customer's mindset** – An important part of curating a digital strategy to improve the customer experience is gaining an understanding of your customers' mindsets. This involves a process of drilling deeper than mere analytics. It requires understanding your customer on an emotive level.

A customer's attitude towards your product or service will give you an insight into their approval rating. Once an organization has an understanding of customer opinions, it is possible to tailor technological advancements to reposition how a product or service is provided. Digital Transformation requires a high level of emotional intelligence from business leaders and understanding the customer's needs plays a major part in driving forward technological changes.

- **Map your customer's journey** – Customers are often your biggest mouthpieces when it comes to spreading the success of any digital advancement. Organizations must focus on the entire customer journey from the initial interaction right through to the point until after commerce. They must also push for customer loyalty and repeat transactions. Customer-journey mapping involves considering the entire customer experience and how an organization can produce a strategy that fits the experience.

"Having a single customer view is far from [having] a guarantee that Digital Transformation efforts to enhance the customer experience will occur. It's the action that matters. Even if all the processes, transformations, skills, mindset, changes, and connections are in place, a single customer view doesn't mean an improvement in the customer experience as such.

The ability to do something with technological readiness is one thing, culture, and ability (or will) to act and effectively do something, is another thing. This requires profound changes and a deep understanding of the customer journey." [21]

- **Know Customer Expectations** – Knowing the expectations of your customer keeps your business agile. With modern technology, customers have set the bar high when it comes to expectations about technology. They expect speed, efficiency, and clarity when using your technology. This is a key driver of Digital Transformation because businesses must make a good first impression on customers. This is especially the case for new technologies. You get one opportunity to display how your technology meets and exceeds expectations. Any delays or misunderstandings will turn customers away very quickly. Furthermore, word of mouth will spread quickly if the technology is not up to snuff. This underpins the importance of accurate and informed testing.

- **Understand the Marketplace** – Understanding the marketplace has two key elements when it comes to implementing Digital Transformation. First, business leaders must have a proficient understanding of their customer make-up, demographics, online behaviors, and online spending patterns. Second, accurate tools and data must be collected to understand the customer so action can be taken fully. The customer experience can help curate the creation of technology that accurately fits the ideal customer, including developing technologies that specifically fit their needs.

3.   Strategic Cost Optimization

Strategic cost optimization within an organization has two key steps. First, this process involves internal investment in the skill and development of staff that are responsible for delivering technological change within an organization. Secondly, it involves a strong recruitment drive that helps maintain and attract the best talent. We examine these two steps that business leaders can implement to optimize the cost of producing new technologies and lowering recruitment costs.

- **Training and Developing Staff** – Employees are integral to the Digital Transformation process. They are the ones who are responsible for initiating real technological change within an organization. It is important that organizations invest in the development of the skills of these employees to keep up with the continued advancement of technology.

"Training is a crucial aspect of a technology rollout as a new system, and application deployments will often fail due to inadequate training and lack of use. The organization should recognize onboarding new technology as a progressive ongoing process, and the investment in training should reflect it." [22]

It is important that business leaders develop the soft skills of staff as well. These relate to the skills that foster and initiate creative thinking. Communication and empowerment are two key skills that employees must possess. Digital Transformation requires bold ideas. Employees need to feel that they are backed up by business leaders to try and test the waters with new developments. Likewise, communication among all employees in an organization is important to develop trust and build a culture that embraces freedom of thinking and ideas. Group training and soft skill development programs can help build this culture in an organization from the bottom up. It is important that these soft skills are driven and encouraged from the top of the organization so that they can trickle down.

- **Recruiting to maintain and attract the best talent** – Attracting and maintaining the best talent must start within an organization. This begins with the leadership strategy. Leaders must foster a digitally savvy environment starting with an openness of strategic goals in the firm; a willingness to test new technologies; and empowering and trusting employees to create new ideas. The flow-on effect from strong leadership around Digital Transformation is that it helps build an organizational culture that promotes digital change.

The more comfortable an organization becomes with digital change, the more likely the employees become comfortable with pushing forward technological initiatives. The culture drives employee behavior and makes 'change agents' more engaged in their work. It also creates an attractive working environment externally, so people want to come and work in an organization. An organization's employees are the mouthpieces for recruiting talent.

Mining giant Rio Tinto is a fine example of an organization that has used its culture effectively to retain and attract employees that are capable of carrying out Digital Transformation. They have created a 'mine of the future' philosophy. They effectively augment people and machine technology together. Unifying them together as much as possible allows staff to engage with operations at the grassroots level of the industry.

For example, Rio Tinto employees have created complex software that projects 3D exhibits of the mines. All employees throughout the organization can easily use and interact with the technology to make environmental and productivity gains in the industry. This increases job satisfaction among current employees. It also adds to the recruitment appeal for those talented individuals seeking to work for a progressive company.

Elements within a Digital Transformation Roadmap Process

Organizations that streamline how they roll out their digital strategy have the best chance of success for implementing new technologies. Yet, what does this look like? To standardize and simplify platforms, applications, processes, and services is a two-step process. These two steps involve integration and automation.

1. Integration – A digital strategy must be integrated. Yet, many organizations fall down at this hurdle because they do not understand what it entails. The best place to start is to look at your current digital output and figure out what technology is converting. Where is your business influence coming from? What technologies do you use that draw in your current customers? This process helps standardize and simplify how you operate.

- **Structure Digital Teams** – Integration and streamlining across processes involves putting all your digital teams on the same page. Ensure that they are all working from the same hymn sheet. Are the teams following the same risk assessment processes? Do project developments follow a consistent method? This allows you to boost your digital capacity across different projects.

- **Measure Success** – It is absolutely crucial to measure the success of technology innovations. This is a crucial part of integration that creates more effective processes. Using data, analytics, and feedback tools to gauge success helps identify and standardize ways to make gains.

- **Create Risk Assessment Plans** – While it is important to have freedom of thinking for Digital Transformation, there must be structure behind it to create effective processes. Risk assessment registers and plans are handy tools that help digital teams structure the implementation of new technologies and highlight any bugs or issues before projects are developed to the point of no return. This saves both time and cost in the long run.

2. Automation – Automation and digitalizing IT as well as business operations is another vital component of streamlining Digital Transformation processes. It increases efficiency in the testing process of new technologies. This can free up more time IT staff can spend on research and development, rather than constantly testing current software developments.

Testing automation significantly enhances the value of digital teams. This is because it hands back the governance of the testing of technologies to developers. It helps testers identify issues earlier and easier. It also helps streamline budget calculations, scheduling, and quality assurance management. Automation reduces the risk of ineffective software testing and increases the effectiveness of business operations throughout an organization.

Operational Agility

Operational agility is another key driver of Digital Transformation. Since technology is so volatile and new advancements are being introduced, organizations must now have the ability to pivot their business operations and move the business in a new direction, if necessary. Importantly, any pivot must happen with speed and efficiency, or organizations risk being left behind by competitors who have adapted to technological change quicker.

"In today's market, not only is change happening quickly, it's forcing businesses themselves to change quickly. It's a constant flow of innovation, disruption — and sometimes chaos — that is moving us ahead, even faster than we ever imagined. Many say agility is the key to surviving in the age of technological hairpin turns. In fact, 68% of companies identify agility as one of their most important initiatives." [23]

What can businesses do to drive operational agility internally? This is where creating an effective, well-thought-out strategy is important. Business leaders must table ideas that can produce operational agility and then follow through with their execution. Agile businesses have the following characteristics:

- **They look to consistently improve** – The most agile businesses are always looking to improve their technologies and their methods. These businesses follow the BTB *"Better than Before"* mantra, which provides an opportunity for growth, adaptation, and ultimately, agility.

- **They improve the customer experience (Cx)** – Agile organizations are constantly asking how they can better deliver their product/service to customers. Enhancing the user experience means that the end goal is always clear. These organizations pivot their behavior and processes to suit the needs of the customers. Businesses cannot afford to lose sight of whom they are serving.

- **They hustle** – Hustling equates to business efficiency. It means having processes that drive automation and integration. Businesses that understand their structures and their goals and that have a clear vision are quick to act and even quicker to find and exploit opportunities.

- **They are fiscally smart** – Digital Transformation can be a bottomless pit if resources are just thrown into technological developments that do not have any thought behind them. The most agile businesses understand where gains can be made and where resources can be pooled. Resources are then pointed in that direction. There is room for creativity, but it is set around financially sound parameters that can be consistently measured throughout the development process.

Digital Transformation consists of several different elements. Organizations that identify the key drivers of Digital Transformation will remain successful in their industry. Understanding the key drivers of Digital Transformation is one thing. Yet, being able to execute the key drivers internally is what separates the digital champions from the rest.

Competitive threat is arguably the most important driver of Digital Transformation. In many situations, it is the one single mechanism that causes businesses to act and behave the way they do. Companies use technology as a source to gain a competitive advantage over their competition. Digital Transformation can disrupt any industry and open up new revenue streams and market segments for businesses that are willing to invest in digital strategy, innovation, and employee skills. Netflix is a great example of a company who has used competitive threat as a catalyst for completely disrupting the traditional viewing platforms.

Customer Experience (Cx) is another key driver of Digital Transformation. The best digital organizations take their cue for developing new digital technologies from customers. It is the customer that dictates where gains can be made in technology and how products/services can be delivered more effectively. In the digital era, consumers are becoming more and more intolerant of digital platitude. Organizations that do not have digitalization as part of their strategy are quickly being left behind.

Strategic cost optimization of rationalizing platforms, applications, processes, and services is another key driver of Digital Transformation. Organizations are constantly looking for methods to streamline their internal processes to more effectively and efficiently produce technological developments. Integration and automation are two key steps that help business leaders implement efficiency. Undertaking the risk assessments, early intervention, and testing allow businesses to become more agile and adaptable to change.

Operational agility is another important driver of Digital Transformation. Organizations that can react to technological changes the quickest and pivot the direction of their strategy and business are the most successful. Operational agility requires a coherent business strategy, a culture that strives to improve and also understands how to improve what they deliver to their customers. Organizations that can achieve these things can drive Digital Transformation and move ahead of the competition.

AWAKEN

Chapter Seven

Barriers of Digital Transformation

Conquer the Culture; you conquer your competition!

Achieving Digital Transformation for organizations requires having a coherent digital strategy, a strong organizational culture, and a close understanding of how technology can meet the expectations of customers. However, it is important to highlight barriers to Digital Transformation as well. It is essential to dissect the roadblocks for organizations that are looking to achieve Digital Transformation and identify what organizations can do to overcome them.

The number one barrier to Digital Transformation is culture. Organizational culture drives digital operations. An organization's culture must have high levels of trust to empower staff to be creative and idea-driven without the fear of failure. Culture falls down when there is dissonance from business leaders between rhetoric and action. Furthermore, if employees do not buy-in to digital strategy, it will be hard to push forward Digital Transformation no matter how effective that agenda may be.

The talent and skill gap are a second barrier to Digital Transformation. Often, talent and skills are a reflection of culture, and the two are interdependent. A strong organizational culture that empowers employees, fosters creativity, and provides strong processes for technological development is more likely to retain and attract top talent. Conversely, if there are cultural issues, organizations will find it harder to retain and recruit the best talent. Overcoming the talent and skills gap requires an investment in those who work in an organization. Business leaders must be prepared to invest time and resources into up-skilling and developing staff. Unfortunately, too many businesses view this as being too costly and difficult, which ultimately affects their digital success in the long run.

Functional and digital silos are also barriers to Digital Transformation. Functional and digital silos occur when groups throughout an organization are separated through a lack of communication and are not prepared or willing to share information with other key stakeholders within the organization. To overcome silos, business leaders must understand the reason why they occur and implement strategies to open up communication channels.

Insufficient budgeting is another barrier to Digital Transformation. A lot of digital technology innovations will push the limit of budget capabilities of an organization. Often, businesses will start a new technological development only for the innovation to hit a budgeting roadblock because of a lack of funding. There are several reasons why this may occur including poor planning and poor testing. To overcome such issues, business leaders must implement strong fiscal and risk assessment policies. This must take place at each stage of development to ensure consistent forecasting and testing standards.

Cyber security is a growing problem and an increased risk to Digital Transformation. The more that companies invest in digital technologies, the more they have to lose at the hands of cyber malware, hackers, and viruses. In some instances, all organizational data is now stored electronically. If that is compromised, organizations may find themselves completely immobile. Organizations must be aware of the cyber security threats that can hamper Digital Transformation and plan accordingly.

Lack of operational agility is an additional barrier to Digital Transformation. Rigidity in business strategy, culture, and processes are debilitating obstructions to Digital Transformation. Businesses must have speed and agility to become and stay digitally agile. This fluidity is reflected in organizational culture. It is the product of strong organizational leadership that empowers staff to drive both creativity and communication.

Culture – The #1 Barrier to Digital Transformation

How digital change can help transform an organization is already well documented. Yet, one has to understand that organizational culture is the main driver of this digital change. Business leaders must be at the forefront of the strategic decisions that drive the culture of an organization.

"Companies need to engage, empower, and inspire all employees to enable the culture change together; working on this disconnect between leadership and employees is a key factor for growth. Those businesses that make digital culture a core strategic pillar will improve their relationships with customers, attract the best talent, and set themselves up for success in today's digital world." [24]

Business leaders need to be proactive in driving organizational culture. Yet, it is also important to break down the steps that leaders can take to improve organizational culture, which in turn drives and maintains digital change. Changing organizational culture is a two-part shift. First, it involves a technological shift that entails:

• Improving processes

• Altering business models

• Delivering an improved customer experience

Secondly, and more importantly, driving your organizational culture towards Digital Transformation involves an attitude and mindset shift which can be much harder to execute. How then do business leaders overcome human variables that can become cultural barriers?

1. Rewrite Company Values and Open Communication Channels – Rewriting company values must come from the top. It involves business leaders recognizing and trusting that an organization requires a shift toward digital change. Furthermore, this shift must be communicated from the top down to all employees. There must be open communication channels that provide fluid conversations and propel an earnest need for change.

2. Visualize the Change – Business leaders must build a vision for change. This requires input from all levels of the organization. Building a vision cannot be forced from the top down. It requires complete buy-in from all levels of the organization. Having organizational input will reiterate the need for change and set early expectations of what the organization wants to achieve.

3. Align Organizational Functions – Once a vision has been created, every organizational department that is affected by this digital shift must align their functions and goals to reflect the changes. Performance measures and KPIs should reflect the overall strategy of the organization and will also provide clarity concerning what needs to be achieved. For example, the marketing team should use data and analytics to measure the success and performance of digital channels in order to recognize where they should concentrate their time and resources.

4. Build Incremental Change – Organizational change takes time. Business leaders should expect initial resistance to change. Transforming organizational culture will require incremental steps in changes taking place that pertain to core functions, before escalating change initiatives throughout the entire organization. This gives employees the opportunity to recognize and familiarize themselves with cultural change. A dramatic shift may induce a complete shutdown or resistance to change that could collapse the Digital Transformation vision entirely.

5. Construct a Feedback Loop – Feedback is central to growing organizational change. It is necessary to have an effective system in place that allows constructive upward and downward feedback. The employees on the front line will practice and implement digital change. They must have the opportunity to communicate to management what is working well and what needs adjustment when it comes to executing the vision.

6. Revel in Digital Wins – A big part of organizational culture involves reveling in the success of digital gains. This helps reward the efforts of employees and reinforces the behaviors that drive Digital Transformation. Furthermore, it provides another source of inspiration for staff to collaborate and execute digital goals within their respective teams.

The Talent/Skill Gap

Another major barrier to Digital Transformation is the talent and skill gap that can occur within an organization. Digital Transformation can have a profound impact on skills and talent management if done correctly. Conversely, organizations that fail to recognize and act on the importance of retaining and attracting top talent will create a very large barrier to Digital Transformation.

"Maturing digital organizations don't tolerate skill gaps. More than 75% of respondents from these companies agree or strongly agree that their organizations are able to build the necessary skills to capitalize on digital trends. Among low-maturity entities, the number plummets to 19%." [25]

Organizations that have not reached a level of digital maturity are faced with the challenge of having to treat the skill and talent gap with the same aptitude and dedication as mature organizations.

What can business leaders do to retain and attract the best talent for a digital change?

1. Drive Up-skilling of Staff on the Job – Up-skilling of staff requires social investment from business leaders. They must be prepared to give staff the opportunity to up-skill while on the job. It is important that up-skilling is done in specific areas that are relevant to the goals of the Digital Transformation strategy. The more experience and exposure staff obtain in implementing digital change, the more proficient they will become in executing and delivering new technologies and projects.

2. Encourage Flexible Learning – It is likely that an organization that is pushing for digital change will be operating under time and budget constraints. This means that business leaders must allow flexibility with regard to when and how they utilize training opportunities. Online learning courses and remote training are great ways to provide this flexibility to staff.

3. Concentrate on Driving Up Job Satisfaction – This is a key point for both retaining and attracting talent. Your employees are your biggest spokespeople when it comes to attracting the best talent. If they are happy in their job, it will attract and entice the best talent to be involved in your organization. Business leaders should focus on driving employee engagement and empowering staff to create, develop, and initiate ideas that can foster technological change.

4. Know the Type of People You Want for Your Organization – When it comes to recruiting new staff, it is often the quality of character that is more important than their skill set. Recruiting staff with a growth mindset and an attitude to match will be able to up-skill quickly and provide long-term benefits to an organization. The best employees want to learn and grow. This is a vital component of Digital Transformation.

Functional and Digital Silos

Functional and digital silos are crucial barriers to Digital Transformation. In effect, these silos are a breakdown in communication that prevents the flow of information across digital and functional teams within an organization.

> *"You need collaboration between multiple different business functions to drive the Digital Transformation. Each function's reason for existing is to make the business as a whole successful – so if they all buy into a digital project and perceive it to be important to the success of the business, you get a cohesive approach and a culture which eliminates siloed thinking and finger pointing when things go wrong. It is about making digitalization everybody's business."* [26]

The consequence of such silos is that key information often does not flow through an organization and it can build resistance to change, a 'them' and 'us' mentality that can divide an organization. The most noticeable digital and functional silos that can damage a move toward Digital Transformation are the breakdown in communication and the resulting lack of flow of information that occurs from top management to the rest of an organization.

Facebook is a fantastic example of an organization that has grown exponentially over the last decade, and that has managed to avoid falling into the trap of creating functional and digital silos throughout the organization. How has a growing organization managed to achieve such a feat?

Business leaders utilized the skills of IT staff around various projects, constantly challenging them to work with different units and broaden their skill sets. This had the effect of starting information sharing across the Facebook staff community, and internal processes become much more fluid because of it.

Facebook lead engineer Jocelyn Goldfein extrapolates this sharing mentality: "On a day-to-day basis, nobody in the company has time to understand what everyone else in the different project teams is doing. But the key thing is to get this rich surface of community and information sharing, in whatever way you can." [27]

Insufficient Budget

Financial constraints are a common barrier to Digital Transformation. It is well documented that investment in digital resources, both software and people, are required to bring about digital change. A lack of planning and failure to consistently measure budgeting goals throughout the progress of innovation projects are a huge barrier to Digital Transformation.

Companies that fail to prepare digital change with fiscal responsibility will find themselves in a budgeting hole at a crucial stage of their digital development. The consequences of poor fiscal planning are that organizations will have to either abandon their digital projects or sink a heavier investment into projects to see them through.

"Digital Transformation doesn't come without investment or without costs, and it takes time to deliver on the promise. But funding for Digital Transformation journeys is particularly nettlesome. Often the promise of a Digital Transformation is some combination of a better business impact as well as lower operating costs. Consequently, executives quickly gravitate to the lower operating costs. That leads them to design short sprints or projects to deliver savings. This strategy often is not realistic for funding the digital journey." [28]

How can business leaders implement effective fiscal parameters around budgeting for Digital Transformation?

1. Form a strong relationship with the financial team – Often it is the case that developers implement technological change. Yet, they can be quite removed from the financial process of budgeting and fiscal responsibility. Forging strong relationships with the finance team and opening communication channels between them and IT sectors helps both groups to achieve progress with the implementation of their digital goals side by side.

2. Create effective budgeting processes – All technological initiatives should follow a similar planning and cost structure, regardless of the desired output. Creating a strong financial framework for projects that are familiar and consistent across all sectors of an organization should be a priority. Therefore, all teams within an organization know the process for calculating the costs involved with any new development.

3. Measure the cost of digital developments constantly – More often than not, technological developments change their scope throughout development. The financial team should carry out mini-audits throughout the development process to assess areas that may be exceeding or overrunning forecast budgets. The members of the financial team are in the best position to seek additional funding or provide advice on where financial resources can be used more effectively. Furthermore, the more projects that are carried out, the more confident the financial team and IT will become in managing budget and fiscal responsibilities moving forward.

Cybersecurity

The advancement of information technologies has opened up how businesses conduct each and every level of their operations. It has brought about many advantages, for instance, increasing efficiency and introducing new technologies that are changing industries. However, the downside to such a reliance on technology is the threat of cybersecurity breaches. These cybersecurity threats, in their own right, have become a barrier to Digital Transformation.

> *"As companies embark on their journeys of Digital Transformation, they must make cybersecurity a top priority,' says Michael Golz, CIO, SAP Americas. 'We have to maintain confidentiality, integrity, and availability of data in all these contexts: on premises, in the cloud, and in hybrid environments."*[29]

The best way to overcome this barrier to Digital Transformation is to prioritize cybersecurity in any conversations from the very beginning of any move towards technological development. It is easier and more cost effective to put in place and safeguard against cyberattacks from the outset, rather than try and implement security measures halfway through the development process. Protecting data of all types should be planned from the beginning of any technological cycle. The steps taken for protection should be constantly monitored throughout the entire digital process.

Furthermore, there must be clear communication between developers and cybersecurity teams. Often, developers begin a new project without worrying about security issues. It is the responsibility of the business leaders that structures and processes are in place to encourage dialogue and a working relationship between these two business sectors from the outset of any project.

Lack of Operational Agility

Rigidity in business operations has a stifling effect on Digital Transformation. In effect, any resistance to change will cause friction throughout an organization trying to implement digital change. A lack of operational agility hampers an organization's ability to maneuver and pivot its digital strategy and respond effectively to technological volatilities.

"Enterprises lacking operational flexibility and agility will be unable to compete, whether against traditional competitors or against new competitors from unexpected sources." [30]

Speed, agility, and fluidity are crucial for organizations to respond to and initiate Digital Transformation. Operational agility affects nearly every other aspect of technological growth:

- It allows an organization to organize quick and effective responses to moves by competitors. If competitors implement new technology, effective organizational agility will allow an organization to either imitate or surpass the technology without losing revenue or market share to competitors.

- It allows an organization to manage employee expectations effectively. Technological change can affect how employees interact internally and with key stakeholders. Operational agility allows businesses to cater effectively to this change, whether it requires an up-skilling of staff or a new recruitment strategy.

- It allows organizations to take advantage of new market opportunities. Changing technologies can open the door to new segments of the market. Operational agility allows businesses to quickly change a previous course of action, and create strategies to take quick advantage of any gap in the market.

- It allows organizations to create new operating models. Digital Transformation requires the adaptation and development of new teams to suit the technology. Operational agility allows the fluid shift of staff and strategy to exploit any digital opportunity.

There are several barriers to Digital Transformation that can cripple an organization's ability to implement effective digital change. Businesses at the early stages of development and maturity are at the greatest risk of running into obstacles. However, effective business planning and strategizing from business leaders can help lead a young organization in the right direction without building a fiscal hole or creating internal friction.

Culture is the number one barrier to Digital Transformation. It is absolutely paramount that employees are empowered to share ideas, information, and communication freely within an organization. Business leaders must put in place strategies that foster this fluidity and also demonstrate to its employees that they are taking Digital Transformation seriously through strong action.

"Talent and skill gaps are a major roadblock to implementing digital strategies effectively. Ultimately, it is the staff at the coalface of an organization that is responsible for driving technological change. Business leaders must demonstrate to staff that they are taking Digital Transformation seriously by investing in up-skilling staff and trusting them to drive their own learning. Creating an organizational culture that embraces digital change will also help the organization attract top talent externally."

Functional and digital silos are the result of a breakdown in communication across business units and teams. Communication breakdowns are a huge barrier to Digital Transformation. This is because silos stop the flow of information, ideas, and strategy that are crucial for executing digital change. The functional and digital silos that are the most damaging are the ones that occur between top management and the rest of the organization. Any dissonance between rhetoric and action, and a lack of communication between top management and employees will only result in entrenching silos within an organization.

Fiscal irresponsibility is another barrier to Digital Transformation. Digital projects have the ability to blow out budgets with exponential speed. Business leaders can prevent such occurrences through sound financial planning from the outset of project development and getting financial teams to work closely with IT and business strategists. The same is also necessary for cybersecurity. The need for cybersecurity is a major threat to digital change because of the amount of data that now requires protection. Cybersecurity teams must be involved in conversations for digital change from the outset to outline processes and measures for protecting company information.

Finally, a lack of organizational agility is another major barrier to Digital Transformation. Rigidity within an organization has the ability to influence any and every other factor of digital change. Resistance to change and reacting slowly to technology can have a detrimental effect on culture and can lead to silos. Furthermore, it can hamper an organization's ability to attract and maintain the best talent. Like all aspects of Digital Transformation, organizational agility must be led from the top down and be simultaneously implemented from the bottom up to achieve universal buy-in from employees who are capable of driving Digital Transformation.

Part Three:
ACTION

Chapter Eight:

How Companies are Using Dx to Disrupt and Remain Competitive

"I'm interested in things that change the world, or that affect the future and wondrous, new technology where you see it, and you're like, 'Wow, how did that even happen? How is that possible?'"
- Elon Musk

Digital transformation involves the development and implementation of new technologies. Industries across the entire business spectrum see the development of new technologies as an opportunity to disrupt current industries as a way to remain competitive and to increase both revenue and market share.

Some powerful companies have been fine examples of digital disruption. These companies have developed new technologies to disrupt entire industries. In the majority of instances, digital disruption has grown from a need to remain competitive in the marketplace.

Airbnb - Airbnb has revolutionized the travel industry. They have totally disrupted how people all over the world manage their accommodation. Their 'home-sharing' company has helped transform the share economy. Ordinary people, all over the world, can now rent out their rooms and their homes to make additional revenue, using the Airbnb online service platform. On the other side of the business model, travelers can book accommodation for virtually any length of stay, all over the world. Airbnb has opened up the market and offers accommodation in both popular and non-traditional locations to offer and in some circumstances are directly contributing to the rejuvenation of struggling local economies.

The most revolutionary aspect of Airbnb is that they are the biggest service provider for accommodation in the world; yet, they don't own any property. Their technology centers on the ability for ordinary people to rent out their home to potential users. The Airbnb platform connects people for booking accommodation, and they take a small commission fee for their service. Without any capital costs or large overheads that hotel chains face, they can use their online platform as a base to springboard their technologies with freedom.

Airbnb used their online service platform to completely bypass other accommodation providers such as hotels, motels, and hostels. In effect, they were utilizing the masses to drive their demand. They are appealing to the same market segment and demographics as other providers. However, it is their unique selling position (USP) as an online platform and their online geographic technology that has truly set them apart. They have repackaged how accommodation is offered. They gave homeowners and travelers a contemporary, speedy and social platform to easily rent and find accommodation.

"Airbnb's formula is very much a logical product of its time. We buy and sell products and services and share our experiences online using apps that are linked to our social media accounts. Technology has come so far that we don't even need to do much research anymore. Your geo-location helps all these digital tools define which specific product or service is nearest to you." [31]

It is obvious that Airbnb has succeeded in initiating new technology within the travel industry. But it is imperative to look deeper to see what techniques Airbnb have developed within their Culture Code to disrupt an entire industry and remain at the cutting edge of digital developments for a sustained period of time.

1. Business leaders understand technology – Airbnb have become an effective disruptor because their business leaders understand the technology landscape they are operating in. This has allowed Airbnb to consistently stay a few steps ahead of the competition when they are operating with a constantly developing business model. The Airbnb founders are designers by trade, so they understand the technology landscape and as a result can easily grow rapport and effective working relationships with their staff. These functional working relationships that are built on mutual trust are necessary to drive digital culture and create a fluid business model.

2. Airbnb actively protect their culture as business scaled – Co-founder Brian Chesky has emphasized a number of times the importance of protecting their entrepreneurial culture as the organization scaled. They prioritized the culture of the organization and did not allow their size to become a distraction. It was a concerted effort to protect what had made them successful in the first place. Their entrepreneurial mindset allowed them to create the disrupting technology. Protecting that culture would allow them to continue to innovate and create technology developments and remain industry leaders.

"Why is culture so important to a business? Here is a simple way to frame it. The stronger the culture, the less corporate process a company needs. When the culture is strong, you can trust everyone to do the right thing. People can be independent and autonomous. They can be entrepreneurial. And if we have a company that is entrepreneurial in spirit, we will be able to take our next 'woman on the moon' leap." - Brian Chesky [32]

3. They focus on employee experience – Airbnb understands the value of their people. The staff that they employ, particularly digital staff, are responsible for implementing technological initiatives. Airbnb recognized from an early stage that their people are the most valuable asset. By managing them correctly, they have become a sustained source of competitive advantage. Airbnb have focused on the employee experience, and that has helped them attract and retain the best talent available.

Airbnb reinvented how Human Resources (HR) operated. The HR team became the Employee Experience team. This team helped create operational agility and drove forward the entrepreneurial spirit within the organization, which have made Airbnb so adaptable to technological change.

"At Airbnb we are focused on bringing to life our mission of creating a world where you can belong anywhere, by creating memorable workplace experiences which span all aspects of how we relate to employees, including how we recruit them, develop them, the work environment we create with them, the type of volunteer experiences we offer them, and the food we share together"
- Mark Levy, Global Head of Employee Experience [33]

4. Communication is a hallmark of their digital strategies – Fluid communication is an effective strategy for allowing the flow of information throughout an organization. It prevents the emergence of functional and digital silos. Effective communication also ensures that there is no disconnect between internal teams, nor between leaders and the rest of the organization. Airbnb has made it a strategic goal of theirs to ensure that internal communication remains an absolute priority, even as the business has scaled and grown exponentially over the last decade. This desire to keep open communication channels, irrespective of what level or what department people work in has supported their success.

"The culture Airbnb has managed to create is underpinned by not only its commitment to its mission and values, but also to its unrelenting belief in honest, two-way communication. A rule they have is that nobody should hear something from a source externally before they have been informed about it internally." [34]

Uber -Uber was founded at a similar time to Airbnb, in 2009, and the two organizations share a lot of parallels. Uber has utilized their digital code to disrupt the taxi industry and have remained an industry leader for nearly a decade. They now operate in over 80 countries, and over 700 cities and that list continues to grow. Uber is another company to disrupt an industry by engaging with the share economy. They are now the biggest global private transport provider, and they don't own a single taxi. (Remember Airbnb doesn't own any accommodation either).

Uber connects people who require transport by utilizing their application technology. Their app provides simple, real-time, efficient services and a paperless system that attracts users. Similarly, to Airbnb, it also offers the opportunity for people to use their own assets, their cars, to provide a service and make their own revenue. It is the business model that Uber has employed that have set them apart from the competition.

"It's clear that Uber is not a taxi company – it's an online platform that connects people. And that's not new either. The peer-to-peer business model is used by many organizations, including eBay, Trade Me, Airbnb, and essentially every dating service. Technology itself is seldom disruptive. If your industry is going to be disrupted, it's going to be by trivial technology combined with

> *a trivial, but effective, business model. And it's likely to be an outsider, a start-up or an organization from a different industry that's not constrained by current industry logic and thinking, that disrupts you."* [35]

So, what has been the driving force behind Uber's business strategy?

Let's examine their culture code to understand how they disrupted the global transport industry through digital transformation and continued to lead the industry through some difficult times by facing both internal and external challenges.

1. Uber has owned their mistakes – It is well documented that Uber has had their own internal struggles with culture and leadership as they have expanded exponentially over the past few years. It is a sign of their resilience and culture that they have recognized where they have made mistakes and looked to pave the way forward. It would be easy for Uber leaders to turn a blind eye to their internal failings. Owning up to mistakes has allowed Uber to continue to drive their technological innovation in a positive direction. They have now adopted a 'lead to excellence' strategy that ensures that this strong digital strategy is led from the front.

2. Uber has identified and addressed areas of staff weakness – A lack of diversity was severely hampering Uber's implementation of their digital strategy. A lack of diversity among staff led to a problematic culture that had the potential to derail and damage Uber's brand. Business leaders have identified areas of inequity within their employment model and have redefined job descriptions and departments to reflect gender equality. Uber now has a strong female influence amongst all levels of their organization.

3. Uber continues to push business model innovation – Uber has used their peer-to-peer business model to disrupt the taxi industry. However, it is important to note that Uber has continued to work on and refine their business model. An important aspect of a successful Dx Culture Code is a continual concerted effort to innovate. An organization that relies on their initial technology will quickly be matched and overtaken by imitators and competitors.

- The way Uber has shifted their business into China, gives an insight into their culture code and their overall operational agility.

"First Uber radically shifted its strategy in China. There are reports it quit the Chinese market, where it was burning cash to the tune of $1 billion a year, but this isn't true. It sold its Chinese business unit to its archrival Didi Chuxing for $2 billion, but has gained a stake in Didi worth an estimated $5 billion and 6 percent of the voting rights. Didi has about 80 percent of the Chinese market and as part of the deal has taken a small stake in Uber's global business." [36]

4. Uber has exploited their 'big data' competitive advantage effectively – As Uber began to scale, it became clear that their technology collection of big data gave the company an exciting opportunity to grow their value. Their culture code allowed for growth in big data that was extremely hard for competitors to imitate, creating a large barrier to entry in their industry.
Uber used their big data collection to model where demand and supply intersected accurately. They could then use this information to pinpoint where Uber could expand into new cities and ensure that the equilibrium between demand and supply was effectively met. Business leaders identified their competitive advantage early and employed a digital strategy that reflected the need to grow their big data advantage.

Netflix - Netflix has utilized a different business model to Airbnb and Uber to disrupt the television and video industry. Netflix has applied an online streaming model and has ridden the wave of Internet digital consumption to disrupt how viewers all over the world watch series, documentaries, and movies. Netflix has dramatically transformed from a DVD rental business to an Internet television giant.

Netflix has a long history. It was founded in 1997 as a business that attempted to disrupt the VHS industry and introduce flat fees for rentals. The business model focused on DVDs in a time when VHS was still the major in the industry. But Netflix's business leaders recognized the importance of understanding and embracing digital trends and they were part of the shift toward DVD technology. This same component of the Netflix culture code allowed them to take full advantage of the Internet disruption as a viewing platform when this technology developed.

"Netflix is the best example of company evolution … over the years technology has dramatically changed, and Netflix always evolved and adapted to the market. When people slowly started to demand to access content via the Internet, Netflix developed a game plan for covering that demand. In 2006, Netflix introduced its online service, and while the DVD market rapidly shrunk, Netflix continued to grow." [37]

So, what has Netflix prioritized in their culture code to drive forward digital transformation?

They have obviously created agility and openly embrace technology. A deeper look at the Netflix culture code identifies exactly how they have continued to be a game changing digital innovator.

CULTURE DRIVES
DIGITAL EXECUTION

EMPOWER EMPLOYEE
FREEDOM AND
RESPONSIBILITY

HOW TO BECOME
A GAME CHANGING
DIGITAL INNOVATOR

STRATEGY HAS
DRIVEN DIGITAL
TRANSFORMATION

BUSINESS MINDSET
IS CRUCIAL

1. Culture drives digital execution – Netflix understood from their inception that it is the company culture that drives digital execution. Often, organizations make the mistake of prioritizing digital change over company culture. Netflix understood that they needed to either adapt their technology quickly or become a disruptor in their own right through the implementation of new technology. Executing these changes were only possible if the culture fostered agility and leaders were prepared to take risks and actioned a disciplined process for creating and carrying out digital strategy.

2. Empower employee freedom and responsibility – Netflix had a concerted effort to give their employees the freedom, responsibility, and empowerment to implement their overall digital strategy. Business leaders were receptive to feedback and communication flowed more effectively when ideas were brought to the table. This allowed the creation of a constantly evolving culture that could respond to opportunities and threats with real speed.

> *"It's not like it's a secret set of rules. It's an evolutionary process. The culture of Netflix is still evolving and always will. The Netflix culture deck was not written as a tablet of stone. It wasn't written for anybody else other than the people who worked at Netflix."*
> *- Patty McCord, Former Culture Initiator Netflix* [38]

3. Strategy has driven digital transformation – Netflix from its inception has had a strong business strategy that has focused on how they can deliver a simpler service to their customers. This was the reasoning behind the introduction of flat fees. It was a simpler business model that attracted new customers to use a flat fee model. As Netflix developed, their strategy continued to drive digital change. They saw DVD's as a more effective and efficient model for customers, so they began to shift their business towards DVD's to take advantage of that opportunity.

The strategy also drove their shift to Internet streaming. Business leaders viewed online platforms as a far simpler model for customers to consume video content. This catering to the customer strategy also brought about the introduction of playing continual episodes that have brought to the fore the *"binge-watching"* of online series. Netflix leaders saw value in releasing episodes continuously and all at once to cater to their customers. Furthermore, Netflix is now creating exclusive content, which caters to an easier and simpler customer experience. The result of having a strategy that puts customer experience at the forefront of decision-making has created incredibly loyal customers and this strong base of users, in turn, has built strong barriers to entry in the online content industry.

4.   Business mindset is crucial – Netflix has successfully created a mindset and an attitude that embraces digital change. Business leaders have created this mindset from the top down and empowered employees to simultaneously build this attitude from the bottom up. The result has been a thriving culture that understands how digital change can improve the customer experience.

"At a crucial moment in its history, Netflix understood this better than most. It set about creating an agile mindset that would allow it to evolve in tandem with the needs of its target audience, and its Culture Deck is famous in Silicon Valley and beyond as a blueprint for wholehearted change. Putting people and culture at the heart of its digital transformation allowed it to innovate quickly and with purpose, disrupting competitors and tapping into fresh market segments." [39]

The rate of technological development is causing quicker and more pronounced digital disruption across all business industries. Airbnb, Uber, and Netflix are three examples of companies that have used digital transformation to disrupt their respective industries. Most importantly, all three companies have also continued to innovate and utilize digital transformation to remain competitive even after their successful disruption.

What is important to note from these three companies is that it is not technology in itself that has been the main driver of digital transformation. Instead, technology has simply been a tool or mechanism for implementing and driving digital change. Essentially, it is the people who drive digital change that has been these companies major advantage. Strong organizational strategy and culture are absolutely paramount for initiating digital transformation.

Airbnb, Uber, and Netflix all have their own unique culture codes. They have found their own way to disrupt their industries and use their own people and culture to their advantage. From an early stage, Airbnb prioritized culture over all other facets of the business. This allowed them to use their culture to shape their technology effectively. From their inception, this has been a sustained source of competitive advantage for them.

Uber has had well documented cultural and leadership issues over the past few years. However, they were able to identify and own up to their mistakes without a damaging, negative impact. Uber understood from an early stage that their management of big data could create a sustained form of competitive advantage, as it was very difficult to imitate. As a result, Uber invested in people who could advance their big data strategy. Their culture code has centered on big data innovation. It has seen Uber use big data to understand the share economy with absolute precision. They now operate successfully in over 80 countries and have recently broken into the hard to crack Chinese market with success.

Netflix understood from a very early stage the importance of tailoring their business model towards the evolving need of the customer. They were able to utilize their culture code in such a way that they were in a position to maximize any shift in consumer preference. Netflix became early adapters to both DVD and Internet streaming technology. Culture drove Netflix's operational speed and agility. This agility then became a source of competitive advantage, as they were able to secure consumers who were early adopters before the competition was ready to move. Even now, with millions of users worldwide, Netflix still relies on their culture code to drive digital transformation.

What these three companies show us is that technology can deliver transformation. However, only people can deliver that technology. Ultimately, it is the culture code of an organization and how they manage their employees that determine their digital success.

Chapter Nine:

9 Hacks for Successful Digital Transformation

"Nuclear power is a young technology - there's so much more to be discovered. That's what makes it so exciting to me. Yes, there are problems, but innovative people are going to be able to come up with solutions and bring the technology to its full potential."
- Leslie Dewan

Recently my kids and I visited Kansas City. We went to the WWI museum, and I showed them all around the city. Yet, with everything there is to see in that town, the highlight of our visit was going to Top Golf.

If you have never been there, you should go. It's amazing. What's interesting is not the fact that you can practice your swing – you can do that in most cities – but it's the technology involved.

They did not set up a golf place with fancy golf cards, but they used technology and gamified the experience.

Each ball has a chip, and each chip is programmed into a system that displays on a screen. You not only have to get it into the hole, but you get more points if your ball makes it to certain parts inside the hole: more points if you score in the center, fewer points beyond it, and so on.

The point is that the digitalization and gamification component of the game attracts and increases the interest of the new generation. It's made for a thriving business in a game that's struggling to find young new golfers.

It's just another example of how a company can disrupt the marketplace by taking something as conventional as golf and transform it digitally.

I'm sure it wasn't easy for Top Golf to figure out exactly how to go digital. Knowing what methodologies to follow to implement Digital Transformation in your organization can be a difficult process.

There is so much information available for business leaders now, it can be difficult to differentiate what will succeed or fail. Digital Transformation involves the process of transforming your organization towards adopting and embracing new technologies to remain competitive. However, Digital Transformation is much more than just technology. More importantly, it also involves managing and motivating people. Driving strategy and organizational culture are two key components to initiating digital change. Business leaders should strive to empower their staff internally. Driving communication, the flow of ideas and information sharing, pushes forward a desirable culture that embraces change and will ultimately determine the overall success of your digital strategy.

Small and medium-sized organizations are constantly striving to become digitally mature organizations. The following nine hacks are particularly useful for early growth businesses that have not yet reached that stage of digital maturity. It is possible to achieve successful Digital Transformation within small organizations without blowing budgets or completely deconstructing how a business currently operates. These hacks involve using the strengths of your business to position yourself to take full advantage of technological opportunities.

Successful Digital Transformation relies on implementing digital strategies in a method that suits the unique selling point of an organization. These nine hacks are so useful because even though organizations have individual needs, the overriding themes of Digital Transformation remain consistent. This means these

Digital Transformation hacks have universal application across industries.

The way that technology is now advancing, every business must take Digital Transformation seriously, or risk becoming susceptible to being overtaken by competitors who are working hard to advance their technology.

Hack #1: Focus on Ease of Adoption

The role of business leaders looking to implement Digital Transformation is to make it as easy as possible to adopt new technology. This process involves having a complete understanding of the customer experience and how you can position your technology to benefit your end users. So, what does this mean? It means understanding how you can utilize technology to deliver your product/service in a better way for your customer. This is a two-stage process:

1. Think about the external customer: This is about tailoring your technology to deliver a better experience to the end user. This is about focusing on the concept of ease of adoption for the end user regardless of who they are. In essence, don't profile your potential customers too narrowly. Identify how you can utilize technology to cater to entire market segments effectively. It may mean that as capabilities grow, organizations can position themselves to deliver different technologies to different market segments.

2. Think about the internal customer: It is also important to consider the internal customers that are involved in the delivery of your product/service. Consider how you can also implement technologies that can benefit how you deal with key stakeholders that are involved in the entire process of creating your own customer journey. Tailoring technology developments to benefit internal customers can open up revenue streams that had not been previously considered.

So, understanding your internal and external customers is critical.

However, it is also important to direct your staff and culture towards a strategy that puts the end user at the forefront of decision-making. Business leaders should empower employees to foster ideas and communication that can enhance the experience for the end user. Often, employees on the front line will be in the best position to understand where technological advancements can be made to make gains.

Implementing an organizational mindset that prioritizes end-users allows the design to occur with the customer experience in mind. It empowers staff to introduce a technological change that is practical, intuitive and familiar. It involves being one step ahead of the user and designing the technology in such a way that will make it easy for users to adopt, without departing from your unique selling point (USP) that has made you relatable to customers in the first place.

Hack #2: Think Holistically About Digital Transformation

Thinking holistically about Digital Transformation is another hack that business leaders can implement within their own organizations. Holistic thinking means making informed decisions on how new technologies can positively influence every aspect of your business processes. So what steps can business leaders take to advance their holistic thinking to a new level?

•   Think about how automation can help you advance your technology. Where can gains be made to speed up internal processes to make your business more agile? This can involve finding interim solutions for manual processes, or a lack of technology, until you are able to put a long-term solution in place.

- Understand what you need to implement from both the front end and back end. Even if this means introducing new technology in phases, have an overall plan for implementing new projects. Business leaders should encourage their IT staff to make small gains in this area. Incremental changes result in a big shift in digital capacity over time.

- Evaluate your existing processes. Find out what areas you can make the switch from manual to automation and how you can create opportunities for your staff to utilize digitalization to become more efficient.

- Try and find a platform that can accommodate the needs of an entire organization. Familiarity in systems will help foster communication between sectors within your organization and improve the flow of information between your supply chain, back office, accounts and top management.

Hack #3: Leverage Gamification and Social Collaboration

It is important that business leaders can convey fundamental information and strategy in an engaging way. This process is known as gamification and involves presenting information to key stakeholders and employees in a way that is engaging and likable. For example, from a marketing perspective, viewing data in an Excel spreadsheet is far less intuitive than seeing data presented in a way that draws in employees and engages them in conversations and action. Marketing teams can use gamification to help organizations understand that they can make a difference by tailoring the way they portray their information. Furthermore, with great planning and leadership, effective gamification can be achieved for businesses with tight budgets and limited financial resources.

Social collaboration can also be used as leverage to help drive Digital Transformation. Social collaboration involves the flow of information, ideas, opportunities and insights within an organization. It involves fluid conversations between employees at different levels and an open-door policy that is nurtured across hierarchies and departments.

> *"A valuable attribute of a high-performing organization is its ability to share insights, engage in thought-provoking conversation, and act in the moment of opportunity and risk. When people work across different departments, locations, and time zones, information flowing throughout the enterprise becomes a critical enabler of those capabilities – transcending organizational structure, decision support, and meaningful employee engagement."* [40]

Primarily, social collaboration begins with top management. It is a strategic decision to build communication and empowerment throughout an organization. Leveraging social collaboration does not have to involve huge costs either. It can be as simple as encouraging employees to share ideas to improve technologies. Business leaders should work hard to gain the trust of employees by reciprocating communication and executing social collaboration strategies through the use of social collaboration platforms.

Hack #4: Create a Solution that Balances Access and Security

One of the biggest challenges of implementing new technologies is protecting the security of data. Business leaders must engage in a balancing act between protecting data and pushing to progress their digital technologies. Enclosing the data is an important component of any digital development. To enclose data effectively, business leaders must ensure that there is an operational process set out to involve security teams from the beginning of any project development. Security processes can no longer be separated from development. Any silos created in this area of an organization can drive up costs exponentially later on in the development, often when it is too late.

"Cybersecurity has become a key strategic priority for digital business and is a topic (along with compliance and data usage) we need to be open about it if we want to succeed in Digital Transformation. Moreover, in order to be able to innovate and realize their digital potential in regards to any given business and customer goal, organizations want security approaches that enable them to focus on their business, a phenomenon which is changing the face of the cybersecurity industry." [41]

Business leaders must be careful not to implement any digital change or security measures in a silo, especially for organizations that are making the shift to cloud-based or hybrid models. Business leaders must come up with an inclusive way to involve the right people in creating an intermediary way to access data. Implementing a phased approach is a great method to balance out the tension that exists between the enclosure and the opening up of data.

Hack #5: Focus on Being Digital, Instead of Going Digital

Business leaders should be process oriented instead of outcome orientated when it comes to Digital Transformation. So, what does it mean for an organization to be process orientated? It means that strategies are in place that concentrate on what an organization can currently control to implement digital change. This involves an emphasis on working with the people within an organization and empowering them to direct conversations towards an end goal.

What can be controlled in the present is educating, preparing and shifting the people and the culture within an organization to move towards Digital Transformation. Up-skilling staff, empowering employees to canvas ideas and new initiatives, improving communication and developing smaller digital teams are all steps that can be taken to 'be' digital.

"Being digital is about using data to make better and faster decisions, devolving decision making to smaller teams, and developing much more interactive and rapid ways of doing things. Thinking in this way shouldn't be limited to just a handful of functions. It should incorporate a broad swath of how companies operate, including creatively partnering with external companies to extend necessary capabilities. A digital mind-set institutionalizes cross-functional collaboration, flattens hierarchies, and builds environments to encourage the generation of new ideas. Incentives and metrics are developed to support such decision-making agility." [42]

Organizational leaders have to be agile enough to respond with a digital mindset to current and future challenges. Directing organizational culture is constant work, but if it hasn't already, it needs to be initiated immediately. Otherwise, too much energy will need to be exhausted educating employees about digital change that could impact both project timelines and delivery of projects into the future. Forcing culture upon employees when digital change is required will not work either. People need time to create and evolve a digital mindset, and this is something that business leaders should be constantly working on from the very moment digital strategies are introduced.

Hack #6: Use Data Intelligently

Having big data is not the same as leveraging it. Organizations should position themselves to use data as a benchmarking tool to make better decisions in the future. Processes must be put in place to utilize data and analytics effectively. Data is often used ineffectively or inefficiently. Organizations often collect too much irrelevant data or are unsure how to utilize the data they do have successfully.

"Business intelligence, and all the concepts that fall under this umbrella discipline (including data integration, big data, data

lakes and reservoirs as well as analytics, as examples) continue to play a strategic role in the digital era, despite its slightly tainted reputation – and are a solution that should be explored far more for the future success of any digital organization. The importance of analytics cannot be overemphasized. Making analytics work for a business has become an imperative in an incredibly competitive and economically challenging environment. Having all the data in the world means very little if the company cannot leverage it towards achieving an organizational strategy." [43]

Organizations have to balance out the collection of data with its use. Processes should be in place to prioritize what data should be measured and how it can be used to create more efficient processes. It is possible to be data rich and yet information poor. For example, data should be collected at every stage of the customer journey. It should then be analyzed to provide the best way forward to make incremental gains with technology shifts. Using data is a great way to identify where organizations can implement automation. Leaders must ask how their data can bring about technological improvements and enhance the overall customer experience.

Hack #7: Architect the Future and Design with Disruption in Mind

To architect the future, is to position and shape everything in an organization towards opportunities. This means disturbing the status quo within an organization, as it is now, to create disruption. When it comes to Digital Transformation, it is important that organizations design with disruption in mind. So how do business leaders implement design innovation?

1. Begin with the customer – To architect the future, an organization must begin with the customer. Design collaboration occurs by combining technology, organizational values, and strategy to meet the needs of the customer. Where these three components crossover to meet the needs of the customer, is where design innovation occurs. This process involves understanding what can be improved in the customer experience process and converting that into technological advancements.

2. Create a design philosophy – IT employees must be empowered with the skills and resources to transfer their technical knowledge into technical solutions. A design philosophy involves top management and the employees capable of producing digital change, working closely together. Top management can provide the overall strategy and IT staff can provide the technical grunt. Together, this design philosophy can bring about technology gains that may not have been thought of in the initial stages of development. A design philosophy creates an element of speed and agility within the business. It progresses and develops an organization's technological resources. It makes it easier for the business to make shifts and adjustments to take advantage of opportunities that present themselves. If customer expectations change, organizations can maneuver their design to match their needs.

Hack #8: Take a Digital and Experiential Approach to Learning

For Digital Transformation to be successful, creating a meaningful digital learning experience should be at the forefront of business leaders' decision-making. It is a crucial element of developing organizational culture. Processes should be put in place to create a digital learning experience for staff that supports all other organizational efforts to be digital.

L'Oreal is a fantastic example of a company that has taken a digital and experiential approach to learning. They made a concerted effort to build a leadership development program that had a real learning focus:

"The top 1,000 executives at L'Oreal have participated in a range of learning experiences, enabling them to build digital roadmaps for their regions and businesses, and to model the behaviors that their team members must embrace to execute on these plans, such as a willingness to experiment, an openness to external partnerships, and more autonomous team structures."[44]

A coherent learning process has allowed L'Oreal to create a strategy that is familiar and successful throughout the organization. They have made a concerted effort to embrace change. By engaging in digital learning, the staffs have challenged existing technological structures and processes which have allowed them to improve on delivering projects ... consistently.

An experiential approach to learning is also advantageous for successful Digital Transformation. Implementing new technologies requires learning and adopting new skills. The more an organization becomes comfortable operating in this environment, the easier subsequent digital change will become. The result of experiential learning is that it helps direct an organizational culture that embraces change.

With the correct processes in place, employees become comfortable adopting new technology. All of a sudden, they will feel empowered to push forward ideas and creative thinking which drives more technological change. The net result is a snowball effect, and Digital Transformation will happen organically as a by-product of the experiential learning. The organization will take on operational speed and agility and will become familiar with change. When businesses see change as being the only constant in their work environment, they can transcend to a whole new level of operational agility.

Hack #9: Develop and Design for Profitability

A large driver of Digital Transformation is profitability. There are constant opportunities in the modern business era to be industry disruptors and the chance to develop and design technology for profitability. Being a disruptor will open up new market segments and help attract new customers to your platform. In effect, if executed correctly, new technologies can successfully create new revenue streams.

Organizations should prioritize design as a way to position themselves to best meet the changing expectations of their customers. This helps organizations to shift the way they deliver their product/service as required. The role of business leaders in this process is to make sure design is a key component of digital strategy across the entire organization – and that design strategies should be created with the overarching goal of profitability in mind:

"Elevate the importance of design. As Apple and Google products infinitely attest, simplicity of design and especially user-friendly end products count for a lot in the digital economy. Successful Digital Transformations are clearly dependent on adoption and usage. To strategy and technology – the two main work streams of traditional business transformations – design must, therefore, be added as a third prerequisite of the digitization effort. The postmortem review of user experience is not the best path to adoption success. End users, whether customers, suppliers, or employees, must help shape the design from the onset and provide

continuous input into the usability and usefulness of any proposed digital effort. "[45]

For design and development to lead to profitability, they must be properly considered throughout every stage of technology implementation. Design cannot simply be considered as an afterthought that only caters to the needs of end users. Using design effectively throughout the customer journey allows organizations to take full advantage of the opportunities presented by both internal and external customers.

Digital Transformation does not have to belong exclusively to the realm of mature organizations. Small and medium-sized organizations can also position themselves to take full advantage of technological gains. By undertaking these nine hacks, businesses can utilize the tools they have at their disposal to become disruptors and leaders within their industry. Even if businesses have limited experience in developing new technologies, they can begin work immediately on transforming their organizational culture to be in a position to take advantage of technological opportunities when they arise.

Digital Transformation is so much more than implementing technology. It involves investment in the people and culture of an organization so that capabilities are built to deliver change. Business leaders should be continually driving employee empowerment, constructive communication and constantly challenge existing norms. Focusing on what a business can do right now, will help build technological change into the future.

Chapter Ten:

Is Your Organization Ready for Digital Transformation?

"The first rule of any technology used in a business is that automation applied to an efficient operation will magnify the efficiency. The second is that automation applied to an inefficient operation will magnify the inefficiency. As we look ahead into the next century, leaders will be those who empower others."
- Bill Gates

Preparing your organization for Digital Transformation requires a coherent plan and clear overall strategy from business leaders. Digital Transformation affects all areas of business. People, processes and technology are all important components of Digital Transformation that are interdependent on each other and all need to be properly considered for Digital Transformation to be successful.

It can be a daunting task for small and medium-sized businesses to plan a shift towards Digital Transformation. It often seems that digitally mature organizations have untapped resources and budgets to implement digital change. It is possible to initiate Digital Transformation by beginning on a smaller scale. By focusing on people, processes, and technology, it is possible for small businesses to create digital waves in their industry.

All industries are now susceptible to Digital Transformation. Over the last decade, nearly every industry has faced significant disruption. It has progressed to the stage where organizations are required to move toward Digital Transformation simply to remain competitive. If your business is just starting out on this journey, or looking for ways to transform to digital, here are the questions you need to ask internally to get your organization ready for this next step.

The impact of Digital Transformation hit home for me when I was asked by Accenture to help their team at the State of California. The problem was obvious from the moment I got on site. No one could make decisions! This group was deadlocked on something as simple as, *"How should we name our internal bank statement accounting rules?"*

I was in a shock. Usually, my clients can make their trivial decisions quickly; it's the big ones for which they need my help. But not here in the Golden State.

Why wasn't anyone making these decisions? After talking with the people there and reading about the project, it hit me. This wasn't a simple case that required reporting a proposed solution to the sponsor of the project, or the board. It was about reporting to the California State Assembly, the state's legislative body.

If the project didn't go as planned, the project team would have to report the situation in front of the state's elected representatives and the state's national and global media.

The stakes were exceptionally high – if California were its own country, it would have the sixth largest economy in the world. Would you like to be the one who had to say you'd messed it up?

The lesson the California team had to learn was simple: make sure everything is well-planned, well-prototyped, and well-proven. But then don't succumb to paralysis. Implement and iterate.

1. Are you prioritizing to "be digital" as a business leader?

It is absolutely imperative that business leaders set the tone when it comes to Digital Transformation. They must lead from the front in their rhetoric and actions. If you want your organization to be ready to implement digital change, you have to show your employees that you are digitally savvy.

Business leaders need to make sure they have the right skills and training to understand how technology is evolving. Are you capable to speak with your technology team about transforming your digital strategy? It is no secret that the founders of Airbnb came from a strong technology background. That gave them the springboard to speak to IT staff as their peers and action Digital Transformation with ease with the appropriate teams. They set the tone for digital change and demonstrated that being digital is a competency.

"Now it is time to transform the boardroom. Digital leadership is not a role; it is a competency. One that every twenty-first-century business leader needs to possess. CIOs (and their teams) need to coach the other leadership teams. They need to be shown the opportunities and issues that come with migrating existing technology and information investment to a model that will serve as your resilient market platform for growth." [46]

2. What is your digital strategy?

It has become more obvious as organizations continue to disrupt their industries, that technology is not enough by itself to drive Digital Transformation. In fact, strategy has more importance in driving digital change. How you manage your people and drive your organizational culture is more important than the technology itself. This is because, it is the people who you employ and work for your organizations that act as the 'change agents'. They have the power to implement the new technology. Without them, the technology remains idle. As a business leader your digital strategy must cover culture:

"What separates digital leaders from the rest is a clear digital strategy combined with a culture and leadership poised to drive the transformation. The history of technological advance in business is littered with examples of companies focusing on technologies without investing in organizational capabilities that ensure their impact." [47]

The most successful organizations at implementing Digital Transformation recognize the relationship between technology and organizational capabilities from the outset. They work hard at building these interdependent components of Digital Transformation simultaneously without prioritizing one over the other.

3.   How will your organizational culture embrace Digital Transformation?

As mentioned above, organizational culture is a key component of Digital Transformation. As a business leader, it is your responsibility to set in place the processes that allow your organizational culture to embrace Digital Transformation.

So what steps can business leaders put in place to encourage a shift to a digital culture?

- **Attack opportunities** – Organizations that operate with the status quo will never find themselves in a position to take advantage of technology. It is the responsibility of leaders to implement a mindset that attacks new opportunities. Business leaders must set the tone to embrace change and move toward challenging obstacles.

- **Focus on the customer** – A customer-centric approach will help the organization prioritize its goals. When you place the customer first, your team automatically shifts into a new way of thinking. By asking how we can improve the customer experience, new ideas and creativity starts to flow.

- **Embrace risks** – Organizations that are risk-averse will never leave their safety net. However, Digital Transformation occurs at the edge of an organization's comfort zone. When your employees are pushed and motivated to change, that is when you will make technology gains.

- **Fail better** – A lot of new technologies implemented will fail. However, you can still encourage your culture to fail better and fail faster. Incremental gains lead to big change. If your staff can learn quickly from failings, the culture will become better equipped to operate in an environment of change.

- **Encourage communication** – Business leaders can encourage communication and a flow of information across the organization by introducing fluid team structures. This removes departmental silos and encourages staff to talk and share ideas. It is the openness of information that allows a culture to grow with transparency. It empowers employees to share and contribute and builds buy-in for Digital Transformation.

- **Build momentum** – The more change that occurs within the organization, the more comfortable people become operating in that space. Digital Transformation is the result of many incremental technology gains. See every technological win as a momentum builder that can transform your organizational culture to become an industry disruptor.

4. Do you have the internal capabilities to execute digital change?

So much talk about Digital Transformation talks about freedom, empowerment, and expression of ideas. However, it is absolutely vital that these components are surrounded with a solid structure to prevent an organization from descending into unorganized chaos. It is the responsibility of business leaders to put in place processes that can lead to Digital Transformation.

Measuring your own internal capabilities requires an honest and open risk assessment of your resources. Several important factors can put your business in a position to execute digital change:

- **Focus on incremental change** – To improve the processes of an organization, it is important that business leaders do not get too far ahead of themselves. Focusing on incremental change allows everyone in the organization to identify an issue and then pool resources together and utilize technology to overcome that issue before moving forward. This allows people to become use to digital change processes without overwhelming them with mass changes.

- **Implement opportunities for innovation** – It is likely that your competitors are already investing in their own technologies. Business leaders must adapt to this changing environment and provide internal opportunities for innovation. This may be something as simple as setting up your own research and development department to create and table ideas.

- **Remember the end user** – Often internal processes become so muddled, business leaders forget why they are in place. Remember why the structures are in place in the first place. Processes that are designed to be as customer-centric as possible should be implemented.

- **Find opportunities to form partnerships** – There are people and organizations out there that have the skills and resources you are seeking. Rather than always fighting against them, seek out opportunities where you can collaborate and form partnerships that are mutually beneficial.

- **Don't persist with what isn't working** – Business leaders must be prepared to stop if any change isn't working. Being able to redirect the business in a new direction is a sign of strength and shows you are reacting to your environment.

5.   How will you retain and attract the best talent?

It is the people of an organization that shoulder the responsibility of executing the real digital change. It is therefore paramount that business leaders have effective structures in place to attract and retain the best talent.

Retaining the best talent requires a level of investment from business leaders. It should be a priority to train and upskill staff continually so they grow in their capabilities. Furthermore, business leaders should empower and encourage their best talent to put forward their own ideas and drive innovation. By removing their ceiling, it will create more motivation for staff to create and embrace digital change. Monitoring industry trends is another way to retain talent. It shows your staff that you are keeping up to date with advancements in technology and shows you are prepared to invest resources to keep your organization at the forefront of the industry.

To attract the best talent, you must have a leadership strategy in place that empowers and encourages your current staff to execute Digital Transformation. It is your current employees that are your loudest voice for attracting new talent. If they are content in their role and continually pushing the boundaries with new ideas and innovations, it will quickly be noticed externally. If an organizational culture embraces digital change it will reflect success to those outside the organization. This will attract motivated, talented individuals and draw them towards your organization. Attracting the best staff should start within:

Google is a fine example of how they attract talent. Their current employees are known for praising Google's flexible working environment that fosters innovation and creativity. Employee empowerment has become a real source of competitive advantage for the organization. The positivity of organizational culture and the fluid organizational structure exuded itself externally. All of a sudden, everybody wanted to work at Google. They became inundated with applications from the most talented people across the business spectrum. By focusing on their culture and empowering their employees, they have been able to create one of the most sought-after working environments in the world.

6.   How will you manage your people?

Managing people through a transition to digital change is one of the most challenging tasks a business leader is likely to face in their careers. With any change, there is likely to be resistance and uncertainty from various quarters as people battle with unfamiliarity. So, what can business leaders do to make this process better and more effective for themselves and the entire organization?

- **Have a Mentor** – It is important that those who initiate the change have someone to turn to. Whether they are external to your organization or you bring them on board for the transition, it is important to have a sounding board for the many moments of doubt and crunch decisions you will have to make.

- **Move on those resistant to change** – Digital Transformation is not for everybody. Business leaders must be brave enough to move on those who are fighting change because they are comfortable with the status quo.

- **Have on board those who understand the need for change** – Digital Transformation may be a generational thing. If you are operating in an industry that is dominated by those who are used to an archaic business model, you should push for those who understand the importance of technology in modern business. It may call for a fresh approach in top management too, which will lead to some hard conversations.

- **Remove functional and digital silos** – Digital and strategic knowledge must be shared across an organization. Business leaders must be prepared teams with agility that can move across functions and departments with ease.

- **Use data people effectively** – Big data is such an important tool for implementing Digital Transformation. Have on-board people who understand the importance of collecting data and know how to use it effectively to make technological gains.

7.   **What is your digital vision?**

It is extremely important that any shift to Digital Transformation should have a clear end goal in sight. Business leaders should make their vision for digital change well defined from the outset. To build a vision, the direction must be led from the top, but buy-in cannot be forced. It requires acceptance from all levels of the organization. Business leaders can set the expectations for digital change within an organization by using three distinct avenues:

- **Through customer experience** – Customer experience is an obvious place to start for setting your digital vision. By understanding how you can improve the way you deliver your product/service through the use of technology, you can set a strong digital vision.

- **Through business models** – Business leaders must understand how their organization will use technology. An understanding of how businesses can utilize technology to their advantage will help define their strategy. Digitally mature organizations could set up their business model to be disruptors. Conversely, small and early growth businesses may choose an attacking or imitation business model until they are comfortable enough with implementing digital change. Importantly, the model must match the current capabilities of an organization.

- **Through processes** – If business leaders see a glaring need to improve organizational culture, they can begin with a process led digital vision. This could involve the improvement of communication to break down silos and the development of internal methods to increase speed, agility, and responsiveness to the digital environment.

It is important that all these avenues receive input from all levels of the organization. Often, it is the employees at the lower levels of an organization that are responsible for the day-to-day implementation of Digital Transformation. It is important to seek out their feedback and understand their viewpoints on how a digital vision can be created, regardless of what the digital vision looks like.

8.   How will you foster innovation?

To foster innovation, business leaders must be prepared to push themselves and their organization out of their comfort zone. It is important for the people within an organization to understand that success isn't comfortable.

"While many IT leaders may feel comfortable with the tangible technical deliverables of facilitating Digital Transformation, understanding the human element of real change across the workforce is a complicated task, and is often, admittedly, out of our comfort zones. But it's a highly necessary one. After all, if modern technology is truly embraced by the people it enables, then the resulting Digital Transformation project's future is assured. Without the support of the leaders and employees who will develop and adopt these innovations, you may as well not implement any change in the first place." [48]

Innovation becomes, in essence, a bi-product of mindset and culture. Innovation will not occur without having a positive mindset and organizational culture that embraces Digital Transformation. Many organizations try and force innovation on their organization without recognizing this point. They will face immediate barriers to Digital Transformation if they try and force innovation on employees without laying the foundation for an appropriate mindset and organizational culture first.

9.   What is your business mindset?

Innovation requires a deliberate mindset shift. Organizational leaders must drive a digital attitude. If they can show their employees that they are willing to push themselves out of their own comfort zone and push forward their own digital learning, the rest of the organization will align. They will recognize the intent and find it easy to follow as they can view the action being taken which backs up the rhetoric. So how can business leaders push forward a change to a digital mindset?

- **Start with the vision** – We have already identified the importance of defining your business vision. Recognizing the social value in this vision is important for developing the right mindset.

- **Bind to and accept the plan** – Business leaders must show they are committed to the plan. Throughout the organization, there will be some resistance to change. There must be solidarity to stick to the plan and let people go if necessary.

- **Actions not words** – As a business leader talk is cheap. By showing your staff how you want your business mindset to be will achieve quicker buy-in, and you will be surprised at the receptiveness of your staff if you are prepared to lead from the front.

- **Be open** – Information sharing is an important component of cultivating a digital mindset. If business leaders make themselves available for employees to communicate with, they will develop trust quickly.

- **Technological change can be broad** – Remember that a mindset shift to digital does not have to be entirely technical. Airbnb and Uber disrupted their respective industries by changing the way the platform delivered their service. It was a common technology used in a new way. Don't think that your organization necessarily needs to reinvent the wheel to be successful.

10. What tools are you going to put in place to implement digital change?

It is also part of your role as business leaders to strategize what tools can be utilized to help implement digital change. Effective tools can help increase organizational efficiency and automate certain parts of the business. Tools can bring down costs and optimize time management. This can often free up more opportunities for research and development. So what tools can business leaders utilize to help them implement digital change?

- **Utilize tools that are already available** – Nearly every tool imaginable has been created for implementing digital change. No matter if you are looking for a technological tool for marketing, sales, accounts or analytics, do some research to find out what is already out there. It will be much cheaper and efficient to adopt technology that is already available rather than create it all internally.

- **Move to the cloud** – More and more organizations are shifting to cloud-based technologies. They improve the efficiency and flexibility of an organization and provide the added bonus of allowing their staffs to work from anywhere.

- **Do not tool dump** – Small organizations need to utilize customized tool solutions. Utilizing tools in a one-size-fits-all formula across the entire organization can be overreaching and create inefficiencies.

- **Use data and analytics** – It is so important to track the performance of your data. Analytics allows business leaders to make informed decisions about technology and improve how projects can be delivered.

- **Implement tools with the future in mind** – Many organizations stumble at this hurdle. They implement tools for right now without considering how they will be used in the future. It is important from a cost perspective that technology is implemented in a way that is maintainable and tools can be utilized now and in the future.

It is possible for all organizations to achieve Digital Transformation. Business leaders of small and growth enterprises do not have to be digitally mature organizations to implement digital change. Business leaders must ask themselves the right questions so that they can initiate Digital Transformation.

The questions I've shared are designed to help you identify how an organization can set themselves up to get the most out of their people. An organization's culture code sets the tone for how well they can adapt to Digital Transformation. It is the people of an organization who are responsible for implementing digital change, so they must be at the forefront of any decision-making strategies.

Digital Transformation is a progression. It requires the right balance of people, processes, and technology. These questions help business leaders understand how these three components are interdependent. Organizations need to work concurrently on collaborating with all three components so that they can successfully bring about digital change.

THE PEOPLE, PROCESSES AND TECHNOLOGY FORMULA

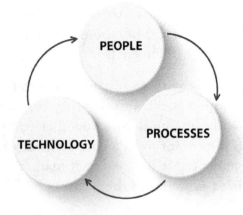

I've shared many insights and examples to help you understand that Digital Transformation is the key to the marketplace of the present and the future. We've learned that lasting organizational change can only take place at the confluence of technology and culture. It's my desire that this book would inspire you and your company to join the Dx movement.

APPENDIX

Digital Transformation Blue Prints Program – Yours FREE $2,500 Gift from the Author

Attention Readers:

Congratulations for finishing this book! To reward you I would like to invite you to become a part of the iTransfluence community of Digital Transformation Leaders. We have created a unique 'Fast Track" program to help you immediately apply the techniques you have learned from this book.

I would like to be clear here. I am giving you the tools and road map to follow to transform your company from an ordinary to a Digital Enterprise, influence your market place and dominate your competition.

Are you serious in your desire to grow? Are you willing to put the ideas and strategies you have learned in this book into action so you can enjoy the rewards of maximizing technology and monetizing the rewards? Then I urge you to take next steps and claim your free $2,500 bonus right now.

To register, all you need to do is go thedxculturecode.com and use access code:

DxCultureCode

Once you register, a member of our team will reach out to you and setup a meeting.

RESOURCES

[1]https://www.mulesoft.com/resources/cloudhub/effective-digital-transformation-examples, accessed Nov. 20th, 2017

[2]Heflo, What is Process Optimization? Steps to Implement it, https://www.heflo.com/blog/process-optimization/what-is-process-optimization/

[3]MIT Sloan Management Review, Strategy, Not Technology, Drives Digital Transformation,
http://sloanreview.mit.edu/projects/strategy-drives-digital-transformation/

[4]Business Insider, Why Google is the best company to work for in America, https://www.businessinsider.com.au/google-is-the-best-company-to-work-for-in-america-2016-4?r=US&IR=T#/#more-than-a-quarter-of-googlers-telecommute-at-least-some-of-the-time-4

[5]The Guardian, Best Practices in sustainability: Ford, Starbucks and more, https://www.theguardian.com/sustainable-business/blog/best-practices-sustainability-us-corporations-ceres

[6]Wikipedia, Digital Ecosystem, https://en.wikipedia.org/wiki/Digital_ecosystem

[7]Ernst & Young, The digitization of Everything: How organizations must adapt to changing consumer behavior, http://www.ey.com/Publication/vwLUAssets/The_digitisation_of_everything_-_How_organisatio_must_adapt_to_changing_consumer_behaviour/$FILE/EY_Digitisation_of_everything.pdf

[8]Forbes Magazine, How a Risk-Taking Culture Enables Oreo's Marketing Innovation,
https://www.forbes.com/sites/johnellett/2014/09/26/how-a-risk-taking-culture-enables-oreos-marketing-innovation/#527ea26c4b0d

[9]CEO Magazine, Embrace disruptive innovation to stay relevant, http://www.theceomagazine.com/business/embrace-disruptive-innovation-stay-relevant/

[10]G C Kane, D Palmer, A N Phillips, D Kiron & N Buckley, 'Strategy, Not Technology Drives Digital Transformation', MIT Sloan Management Review, (2015),
http://sloanreview.mit.edu/projects/strategy-drives-digital-transformation/

[11]Newman, D, 'Who needs to lead digital transformation in 2017', Forbes Magazine, (2017), https://www.forbes.com/sites/danielnewman/2017/01/21/who-needs-to-lead-digital-transformation-in-2017/#525d58988e0a

[12]Get with the Future, '5 Inspiring examples of Digital Technology for Business' The Social Driver Blog, (2013), https://socialdriver.com/2013/07/24/5-inspiring-examples-of-digital-technology-for-business/

[13]Afzal, D, 'The Road of the Future: Top Down Vision in Digital Transformation', Digitalist Magazine, (2017), http://www.digitalistmag.com/customer-experience/2017/07/21/road-oftfuture-top-down-vision-in-digital-transformation-05218565

[14]McKendrick, J, 'Digital Transformation Is Coming From The Bottom Up, Survey Shows' Forbes Magazine, (2017), https://www.forbes.com/sites/joemckendrick/2017/01/31/digital-transformation-is-coming-from-the-bottom-up-survey-shows/#352379ee7b40

[15]Haslam, T, 'Top Down or Bottom Up? Audit Blog, OAG, (2013), https://blog.oag.govt.nz/social-media-audit/down-or-up

[16]G C Kane, D Palmer, A N Phillips, D Kiron & N Buckley, 'Aligning the Organization for its Digital Future', MIT Sloan Management Review, (2016), http://sloanreview.mit.edu/projects/aligning-for-digital-future/

[17]Burnson, P, 'Asia Pacific Leaders Must Become 'Digital Evangelists'', Logistics Management, (2017), http://www.logisticsmgmt.com/article/asia_pacific_business_leaders_must_become_digital_evangelists

[18]Monsanto company history, https://monsanto.com/company/history/

[19]Information Age, 'Digital Transformation 'driven by increasing competitive threats rather than innovation' (2017), http://www.information-age.com/digital-transformation-driven-threats-innovation-123468970/.

[20]Business.com, Digital Disrupt: What We Can All Learn From The Netflix

Model, (2017), https://www.business.com/articles/digital-disrupt-what-we-can-all-learn-from-the-netflix-model/

[21]I-scoop, 'Digital Transformation, the customer experience and marketing' (2016), https://www.i-scoop.eu/digital-transformation/digital-transformation-customer-experience-marketing/

[22]Sharp, J, 'Digital Transformation: The tables are turned', Training Journal, (2017), https://www.trainingjournal.com/articles/opinion/digital-transformation-tables-are-turned

[23]Newman, D, 'Agility is the Key to Accelerating Digital Transformation' Forbes. com, (2017),
https://www.forbes.com/sites/danielnewman/2017/04/18/agility-is-the-key-to-accelerating-digital-transformation/#567bd9d47277

[24]Shepherd, A, 'Cultural change is the main barrier to digital transformation, says Capgemini'ITPro, (2017),
http://www.itpro.co.uk/strategy/28804/cultural-change-is-the-main-barrier-to-digital-transformation-says-capgemini

[25]G C Kane, D Palmer, A N Phillips, D Kiron & N Buckley, 'Strategy, Not Technology Drives Digital Transformation', MIT Sloan Management Review, (2015),
http://sloanreview.mit.edu/projects/strategy-drives-digital-transformation/

[26]Krishnamoorthi, R, 'The 10 pitfalls of digital transformation - #5: Avoid silos and make digital transformation everyone's business', Fujitsu, (2017), http://blog.global.fujitsu.com/the-10-pitfalls-of-digital-transformation-5-avoid-silos-and-make-transformation-everyones-business/

[27]iMeetCentral, "The Silo Effect' puts your business to the test', (2016), https://imeetcentral.com/the-silo-effect-puts-your-business-to-the-test

[28]Bendor-Samuel, P, 'Budgeting Is A Big Constraint In Digital Transformation' Forbes Magazine, (2017), https://www.forbes.com/sites/peterbendorsamuel/2017/06/22/budgeting-is-a-big-constraint-in-digital-transformation/#3406ae2eafff

[29]MIT Technology Review, 'Cybersecurity in the Age of Digital Transformation', (2017), https://www.technologyreview.com/s/603426/cybersecu-

rity-in-the-age-of-digital-transformation/

[30]ICT News Dach, 'Operational Agility Drives Digital Business Efforts –But What About IT?' (2016), http://research.isg-one.de/research/ict-news-dach/news/operational-agili-ty-drives-digital-business-efforts-but-what-about-it.html

[31]Cruikshank, S, 'Is Airbnb Really Disrupting the Hotel Industry? A Look Behind the Scenes', Stormid, (2017), https://blog.stormid.com/2017/05/is-airbnb-disrupting-the-hotel-indus-try/

[32]Chesky, B, 'Don't Fuck up the Culture', Medium, (2014), https://medi-um.com/@bchesky/dont-fuck-up-the-culture-597cde9ee9d4

[33]Morgan, J, 'The Global Head Of Employee Experience At Airbnb On Why They Got Rid Of Human Resources' Forbes.com, (2016), https://www.forbes.com/sites/jacobmorgan/2016/02/01/global-head-employee-experi-ence-airbnb-rid-of-human-resources/#37568ae7c4e9

[34]Growthitude, 'Digital Strategy; It's about company culture' (2017), http://growthitude.com/digital-strategy-company-culture/

[35]PWC Digital, 'Uber, digital and disruption: what's happening and why does it work?' https://digital.pwc.co.nz/ideas/uber-digital-and-disruption-whats-happen-ing-and-why-does-it-work/

[36]Turner, A, 'Top 7 lessons from Uber's strategic shifts' TMForumInform, (2016), https://inform.tmforum.org/features-and-analysis/2016/08/top-7-lessons-ubers- strategic-shifts/

[37]Cloudnames, 'How Netflix transformed from DVD rental to Global Internet TV, (2017), http://cloudnames.com/en/blog/how-netflix-transformed-from-dvd-rental-to-global-internet-tv/

[38]Fastcompany.com, 'She created Netflix's Culture And It Ultimately Got Her Fired', (2016), https://www.fastcompany.com/3056662/she-created-netflixs-culture-and-it-ultimately-got-her-fired

[39]Tappin, I, 'Why culture is key in the era of Digital Transformation' Accenture, (2017),
https://www.accenture-insights.nl/en-us/articles/why-culture-key-era-digital-transformation

[40]Hernandez, D, 'Social Collaboration: Why Digital Transformation Is Not Complete Without It',Digitalist Mag, (2016),
http://www.digitalistmag.com/future-of-work/2016/10/03/social-collaboration-why-digital-transformation-is-not-complete-without-it-04532473

[41]I-Scoop, 'Cybersecurity: security risks and solutions in the digital transformation age', (2016),
https://www.i-scoop.eu/cyber-security-cyber-risks-dx/

[42]Dorner, K, & Edelman, D, 'What Digital really means', Mckinsey.com, (2017),
https://www.mckinsey.com/industries/high-tech/our-insights/what-digital-really-means

[43]Mawson, N, 'Using Data Intelligently' Web brainstorm, Business Technology Magazine, (2017),
http://www.brainstormmag.co.za/features/12834-using-data-intelligently

[44]Chopra-McGowan, A, & Henretta, D, '5 Ways to Help Employees Keep Up With Digital Transformation', Harvard Business Review, (2017),
https://hbr.org/2017/09/5-ways-to-help-employees-keep-up-with-digital-transformation

[45]Booth, A., Mohr, N., & Peters, P, 'The digital utility: New opportunities and challenges', McKinsey.com,
https://www.mckinsey.com/industries/electric-power-and-natural-gas/our-insights/the-digital-utility-new-opportunities-and-challenges

[46]McCormack, A, '9 Steps to Leading Digital Transformation', Connected Futures,
http://www.connectedfuturesmag.com/a/S15A28/9-steps-to-leading-digital-transformation/#.WfbYWEyjLq0

[47]G C Kane, D Palmer, A N Phillips, D Kiron & N Buckley, 'Strategy, Not Technology Drives Digital Transformation', MIT Sloan Management Review, (2015),

http://sloanreview.mit.edu/projects/strategy-drives-digital-transforma-tion/

[48]Weston, C, 'The real challenge for digital transformation is not your tech-nology', CIO from IDG, (2017), https://www.cio.com/article/3211893/careers-staffing/the-real-chal-lenge-for-digital-transformation-is-not-your-technology.html

www.ingramcontent.com/pod-product-compliance
Lightning Source LLC
LaVergne TN
LVHW022340060326
832902LV00022B/4155